Test your Biology Questions

By the same authors

C. J. Clegg
   Anatomy and Activities of Plants (with Gene Cox)
   Lower Plants: Anatomy and Activities of Non-flowering Plants and their Allies

A. E. Pound
   Concise Biology
   Ordinary Level Revision Tests in Biology

© C. J. Clegg 1983

First published 1983
by John Murray (Publishers) Ltd
50 Albemarle Street, London W1X 4BD
Reprinted 1986

All rights reserved.
Unauthorised duplication
contravenes applicable laws

Set in Singapore by Colset Pte Ltd
Printed in Hong Kong by Wing King Tong Ltd

British Library Cataloguing in Publication Data

Clegg, C.J
  Test your biology
  1. Biology — Problems, exercises, etc.
  I. Title   II. Pound, A.E.
  574'.076   QH316

ISBN 0 7195 3863 7

Test your Biology Questions

C.J. Clegg & A.E. Pound

John Murray

CONTENTS

Preface	(iii)
1. Characteristics of living things	1
2. Variety of living things	1
3. The nature of protoplasm and the chemicals of life	3
4. Looking at cells: cell organelles	4
5. Movement in and out of cells	
(i) diffusion	6
6. (ii) osmosis; plasmolysis	8
7. (iii) active uptake	10
8. Cells, tissues and organs; division of labour between cells	11
9. Flowering plants: external structure	12
10. Anatomy of stem, leaf and root	13
11. Skeletons	15
12. Teeth	17
13. Photosynthesis	19
14. Translocation and transpiration	21
15. Mineral nutrition	23
16. Soil	24
17. Carbohydrates, fats and proteins as foods	28
18. Balanced diet: water, vitamins, minerals and roughage	30
19. Enzymes	30
20. Feeding and digestion	32
21. Absorption and assimilation	35
22. Blood and lymphatic systems	37
23. Respiration, aerobic and anaerobic; gaseous exchange	41
24. Homeostasis	46
25. The skin and body temperature control	46
26. Excretion; kidney structure and function	47
27. Sensitivity	50
28. The nervous system and sense organs; the reflex arc	53
29. Co-ordination by nerves and hormones; behaviour	57
30. Movement; muscles and joints	58
31. Growth	60
32. Secondary thickening in plants; perennation and hibernation	62
33. Reproduction; cell division, replicative and reductive	63
34. Flower structure; pollination, fertilisation, fruit formation	66
35. Seed dispersal; seed germination	69
36. Sexual reproduction in vertebrates; embryology; childbirth; parental care	74
37. Simple green plants: *Spirogyra* and *Pleurococcus*	76

38.	Common mould fungi: *Mucor*	78
39.	Mosses and ferns; conifers	79
40.	Single-celled (acellular) animals: *Amoeba*	80
41.	Coelenterates: *Hydra*	81
42.	Parasitic worms: *Taenia*	82
43.	Segmented worms: *Lumbricus* (Earthworm)	82
44.	Insects	83
45.	Fish	86
46.	Amphibia; the frog	87
47.	Birds	88
48.	Mammals	89
49.	Parasitism, mutualism (symbiosis) and commensalism	90
50.	Saprophytic organisms; the cycling of carbon and nitrogen in nature	92
51.	Ecology; man & the environment	94
52.	Health & disease; food preservation	96
53.	Genetics	97
54.	Evolution; the work of Darwin	100
55.	Biological illustrations: an exercise in observation, identification and interpretation	102

PREFACE

This book of structured short-answer questions covers all major topics in the GCSE syllabuses, and their equivalent outside the UK. In keeping with the GCSE National Criteria for Biology the tests assess not only knowledge and comprehension of biological concepts, facts and of their applications, but also the techniques of biological enquiry. The emphasis is on a practical approach to biology, and many of the items pay particular attention to the personal, social, environmental, economic and technological aspects of biology today. Teachers of GCSE biology will find it an invaluable source of test items for differentiated assessment papers.

During the past decade there have been a steady stream of changes both in the content of school biology syllabuses and in approaches to pupil assessment. This book is a response to the trend towards questions that can be marked objectively and which permit a wider coverage of syllabus topics in examinations. In detail as well as in general plan the book represents a response to some of the more progressive approaches to biology teaching without abandoning the advantages of traditional methods:

1. The questions are framed to test knowledge gained from factual learning and understanding gained by experience of experimentation and enquiry.
2. Understanding of many of the concepts and topics is tested in more than one section, so avoiding the rigid compartmentalisation of information that can mar pupils' learning.
3. The section of photographs is an exercise in observation, identification and interpretation which – irrespective of examination syllabuses – should be useful to all students. Elsewhere in the book some selection will be needed to fit it to the requirements of a particular syllabus.

Although some of the items are immediately applicable to the work of candidates expected to attain GCSE grades D and below, mostly they will have to be adapted to differentiate at this lower level of work. Since there is also every need to make provision for very able students this book contains a proportion of items – each with the question number enclosed within square brackets – that will stretch and reward those who have mastered the language and concepts of more advanced biology.

The items have been carefully considered by Donald and Enid Walton and by John Barker, and we are most grateful to them for their thoughtful assistance and for the benefit of their professional judgement. Nevertheless, any remaining errors are ours alone.

C.J.C.
July, 1986.

1 Characteristics of living things

1.1 All living things respire. Name FOUR other processes carried out by all plants and animals.

1.2 Where does respiration occur in living things?

1.3 Which of the following statements are CORRECT?

   A The best indication of the real growth of an organism is an increase in its fresh-weight.
   B Most animals grow until mature whereas plants usually continue growth throughout life.
   C Animal movements are usually slow growth movements involving only parts of their bodies.
   D The removal from the body of waste products of tissue metabolism is a process biologically different from the disposal of undigested food by an animal.
   E Catabolism is the build-up of complex compounds in the organism from simple raw materials.

1.4 For those statements in question 1.3 which you find are incorrect, how would you most simply restate them correctly?

1.5 Name TWO physiological processes carried out by a live mammal but not by a living green plant.

1.6 Name ONE process which occurs in living terrestrial green plants but not in live animals.

2 Variety of living things

2.1 Scientific names of organisms may be difficult to pronounce and to remember. Why are they useful to scientists?

2.2 What is the scientific name for the human?

2.3 Scientific classification sorts organisms into very large groups and then subdivides these groups into smaller units. Place the following terms into correct sequence:

   phylum (or division), genus, kingdom, family, species, class.

2 Variety of living things

2.4 The pie-chart below shows the relative numbers of certain groups of animals.

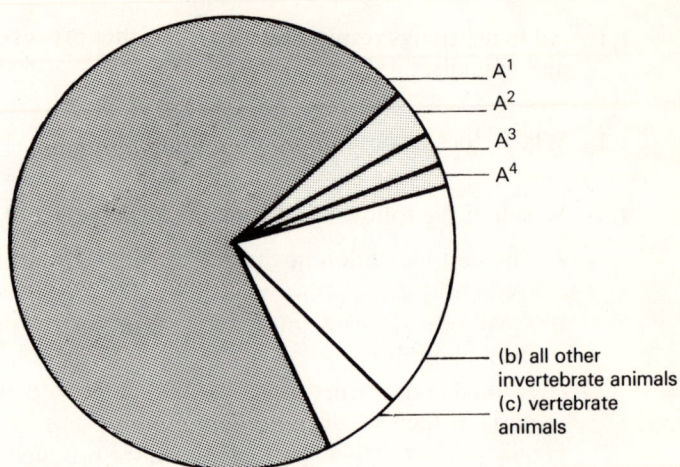

(a) Most animals make up one phylum that is represented here by (A¹), (A²), (A³) and (A⁴). What is the name of this phylum?

(b) What type of skeleton do these animals possess?

(c) What is the name of the largest group of animals, (A¹), within this phylum?

(d) By what three characteristics is group (A¹) distinguished from the members of the other three groups (A²), (A³) and (A⁴).

(e) Name one group of animals represented by (A²), (A³) or (A⁴).

(f) Group (b) represents all other invertebrate animals. Name two phyla of animals from this grouping.

(g) Group (c) represents vertebrate animals. What five groups of animals are vertebrates divided into?

(h) Copy the table below and complete it by naming the two groups of vertebrate animals that maintain a constant body temperature, and by stating the external insulating layer grown on their skin.

Vertebrate with constant body temperature	External insulating layer

2.5 The many different types of plants are listed in the table opposite, together with lettered summary statements. Copy the table and complete it by selecting the letter representing the most appropriate summary, and insert this in the box beside each group.

lichens	
flowering plants	
mosses and liverworts	
fungi	
ferns and horsetails	
conifers	
algae	

A Green plants without true roots, and without water-conducting cells; usually occurring in damp places; producing capsules that release spores.
B Plants composed of algae and fungi living together in close association.
C Green plants with roots, stem and leaves; forming and releasing spores from the underside of leaves.
D Green plants with stems, leaves and roots; producing flowers and seeds.
E Plants producing no green colouring matter (chlorophyll) and living on dead matter or on other living things.
F A very large group of plants generally growing in water; not divided into stem, leaf and root; occurring in various colours.
G Woody plants producing seeds in cones.

3 The nature of protoplasm, and the chemicals of life

3.1 A fully-grown organism has more living substance (protoplasm) than a young one. What is the source of living protoplasm?

3.2 The living cell is said to consist of the nucleus surrounded by cytoplasm. What happens to the cytoplasm if the nucleus is artificially removed?

[3.3] A few mature cells can survive for a limited period of time without a nucleus. Name one plant cell and one animal cell that does this.

3.4 What is the role of the surface membrane in the living cell?

[3.5] State one chemical or group of chemicals known to be harmful to protoplasm and specify what type of damage occurs.

4 Looking at cells; cell organelles

3.6 The nucleus is said to control the whole cell. How does the nucleus do this?

3.7 Apart from the nucleus and the cell membrane the cell contains other sub-units or organelles. Name the organelles associated with the processes of:
(a) respiration
(b) photosynthesis
(c) protein synthesis.

3.8 (a) One chemical substance makes up about 80 per cent of all cells and organisms. Which chemical is this?
(b) Apart from mineral salts, vitamins and growth factors, cytoplasm also contains a considerable quantity of three other types of compound. Which are these?

3.9 Name the insoluble chemical compounds that are stored in:
(a) a liver cell, and
(b) a potato tuber cell.

[3.10] Which two types of chemical are contained in the cell membranes?

3.11 What name is given to the catalysts that assist in chemical changes in the cell, and from what chemical compounds are they made?

3.12 Vacuoles are cavities which may be present in cytoplasm, particularly in plant cells. What are vacuoles usually filled with?

4 Looking at cells; cell organelles

4.1 Examine the diagram of the school compound microscope, opposite and make a list of the labels shown by the numbers 1–8.

4.2 Put the following steps in setting up a microscope with slide for viewing into the correct sequence:

A Select the medium objective lens (×10) or the lower-powered of the two objective lenses (with short, broad lens mount). Turn the coarse focusing knob to bring this lens as close to the slide as possible.

B With the part of the specimen to be examined in detail in the centre of the field of view, swivel the nosepiece (revolving turret) round so that the high power objective lens (long, narrow lens mount) is in line. Look down the eyepiece and focus with the fine-focus knob.

Looking at cells; cell organelles 5

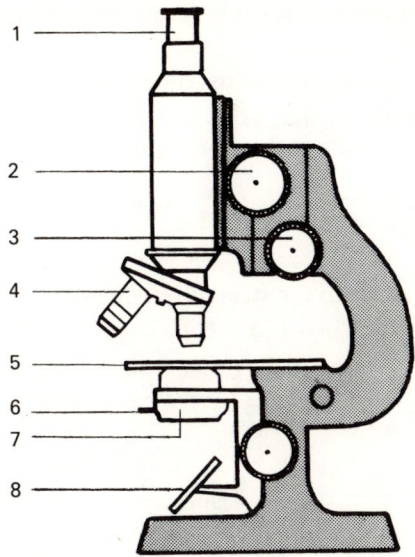

C Arrange the light source to reflect light towards the stage. Check the adjustment of the condenser (to be as high as it will go). Check that the iris diaphragm is about half open. Place the slide on the stage with the specimen for examination near the centre of the hole.

D Look through the eyepiece and turn the focusing knob to move the objective lens away from the slide until the object comes in focus.

4.3 Make a list of the labels to the structures numbered 1–8 in the drawings of generalized plant and animal cells.

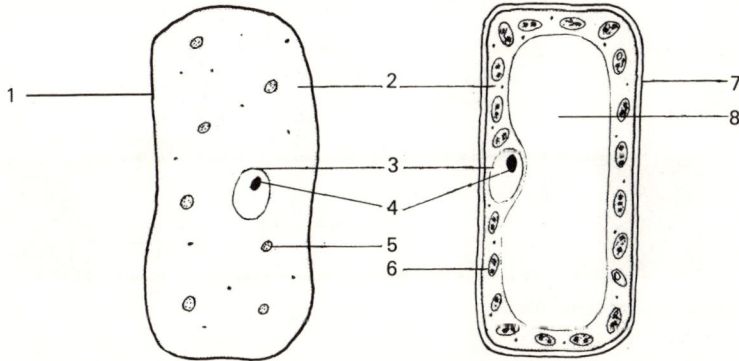

4.4 State two differences in the behaviour or functioning of living plant and living animal cells which may be linked to differences in cell structure.

4.5 What is macerated plant material?

6   Movement in and out of cells: (i) diffusion

4.6 Since the 1930s it has been possible to observe cell fine-structure using the electron microscope.

(a) In what way is this advantageous to the study of cell structure?

[(b)] State TWO problems that arise in electron microscopy because of the nature of an electron beam in relation to the cell.

4.7 What is meant by the term *organelle*?

[**4.8**] Make a list of the labels to the structures numbered 1–8 in the drawing of a generalized animal cell as seen by electron microscopy.

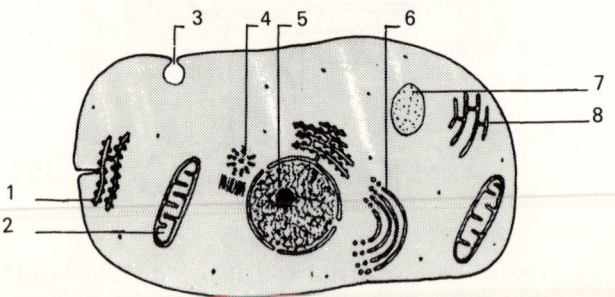

5 Movement in and out of cells: (i) diffusion

5.1 At the start of an experiment, pieces of damp red litmus paper were placed in the centre of a glass tube and at intervals from the centre along to one end. At the opposite end of the tube was placed a small piece of cotton-wool to which a few drops of very concentrated ammonia solution were added. The tube was clamped horizontally under constant temperature conditions, sealed with bungs at both ends, and observed carefully over a 15–20 minute period.

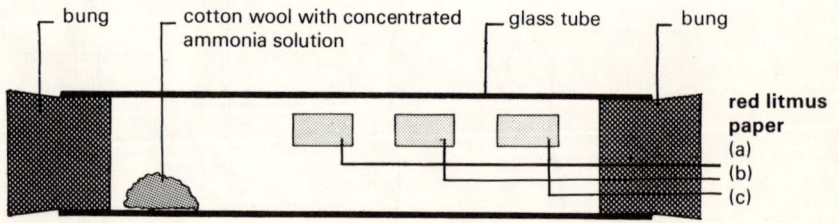

Diffusion of ammonia

(a) What effect will ammonia gas have on damp red litmus paper?

(b) Why must the paper be damp for a change to occur?

(c) How do the litmus papers along the tube at (a), (b) and (c) change with time, during the course of the experiment?

(d) In what way can the ammonia gas reach the litmus paper?

(e) Why was the tube fitted with bungs and clamped horizontally under constant temperature conditions?

[5.2] The diagram represents the *start* of an experiment to investigate the diffusion of different gases:

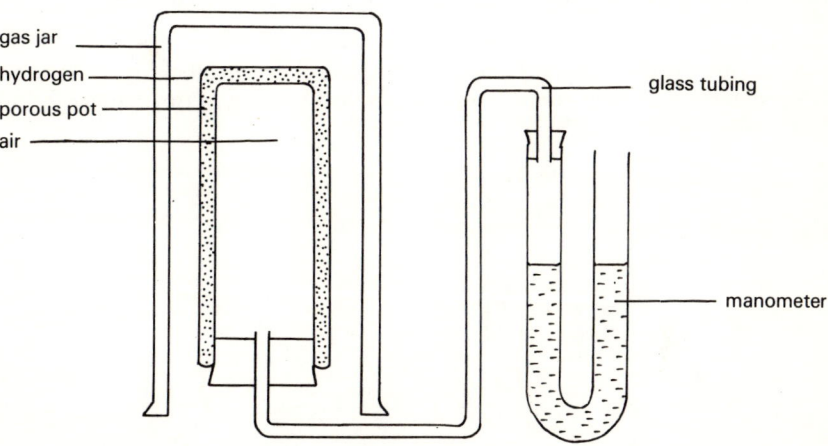

(a) What visible change would you expect?
(b) Give a reason for your answer to (a).

5.3 At the start of the experiment iodine solution was added to the distilled water, sufficient to turn the water pale yellow. The experiment was observed for ten minutes.

(a) What colour change occurs when iodine solution and starch suspension are mixed?

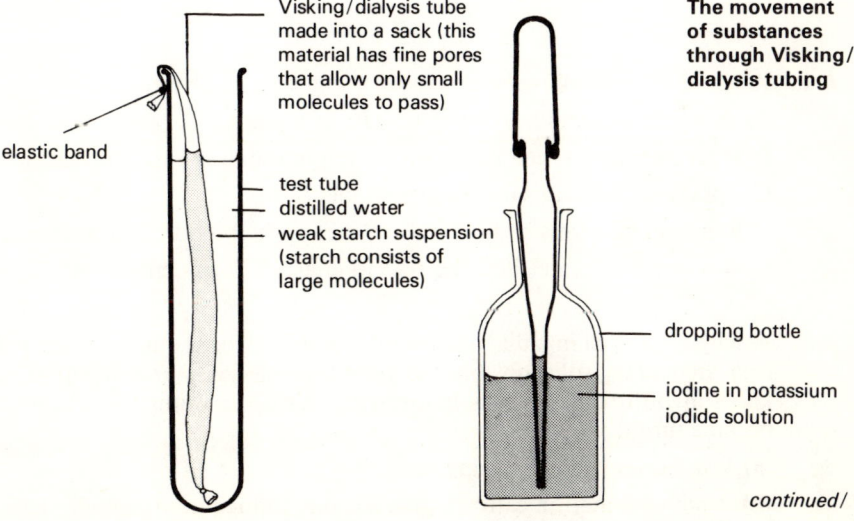

continued/

8   Movement in and out of cells: (ii) osmosis, plasmolysis

(b) After 10 minutes what colour change would you expect to observe:
 (i) in the water in the glass tube
 (ii) in the starch solution in the Visking/dialysis tube?
(c) Give reasons for your answers to (ii).

5.4 Give an example of diffusion through liquid in a living cell.

5.5 Copy the diagrams (a) and (b), complete them by labelling the structures indicated, and insert arrows to show where diffusion of three different substances takes place in each.

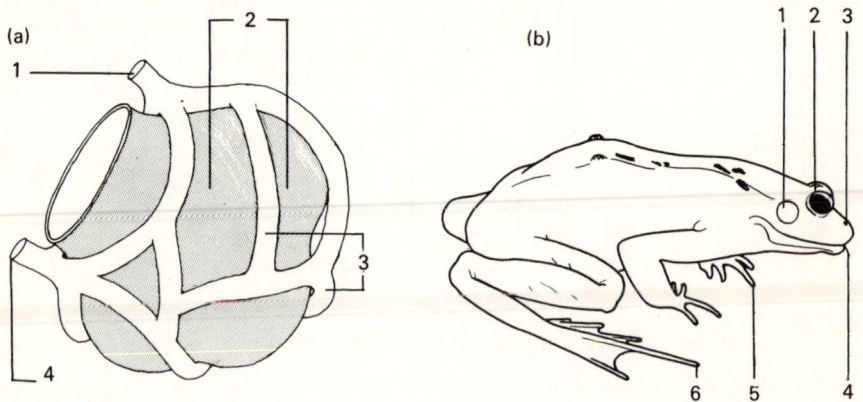

Part of a mammal's lung   Adult frog: external features

6 Movement in and out of cells: (ii) osmosis, plasmolysis

6.1 In which of the following processes is osmosis involved?
A Movement of water into a root hair of a plant.
B Movement of oxygen into a blood cell in the lung capillary network.
C Uptake of mineral salts by plant roots.
D Removal of excess sodium chloride from the blood in the kidneys.
E Movement of water into the flaccid guard cells in a green leaf in the light.

6.2 A length of Visking/dialysis tubing, that had been partly filled with concentrated sugar solution, had air bubbles squeezed out and was sealed with knots at both ends. It was immersed in distilled water for 30 minutes and became turgid.
(a) What does 'turgid' mean?
(b) What explanation can you give for this change in the tubular bag?

(c) What change might occur if the bag is returned to distilled water for a further 60 minutes? Give your reason.

6.3 (a) Define osmosis.

(b) Copy the diagram, which represents a membrane, a solution and the solvent, and annotate it to illustrate the process of osmosis.

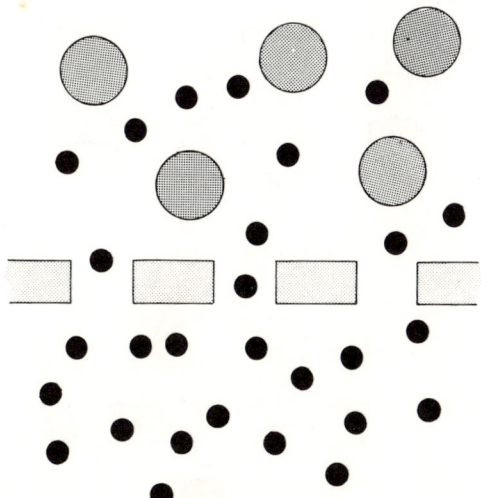

6.4 Cylinders of tissue were punched with a cork borer from the centre of an uncooked potato, cut into 50-mm lengths, washed in running water, and then immersed, two cylinders per tube, in three different concentrations of sucrose solution in test tubes labelled A, B and C. After overnight immersion the cylinders of tissue were withdrawn and each was remeasured to detect length changes. It was found that:
  (i) from tube A the tissue cylinders were shorter and were flaccid,
  (ii) from tube B the tissue cylinders had increased in length and were turgid,
  (iii) from tube C the tissue cylinders were exactly the same length, i.e. 50 mm.

(a) Why were two cylinders used per tube, rather than one?
(b) Why is tissue from a cooked potato not used in this experiment?
(c) What do you conclude about the sugar solutions in tubes A, B, and C?

6.5 Explain why half a cucumber becomes soft if left lying on a kitchen shelf for a few days, but becomes turgid again if its cut end is placed in water.

6.6 (a) Draw and label a plasmolysed cell

(b) What conditions are essential for a plasmolysed cell to become deplasmolysed?

10 Movement in and out of cells: (iii) active uptake

6.7 Meat can be preserved by soaking it in strong salt solution and then packing it in salt. How does this prevent bacteria from decaying the meat?

6.8 What happens to a fungal spore that germinates after landing on recently cooled jam that is made by boiling fruit with its own weight of sugar?

6.9 (a) State concisely exactly where water may enter and leave the cells of *Spirogyra* and *Amoeba*.
(b) In which does the water cause turgor?

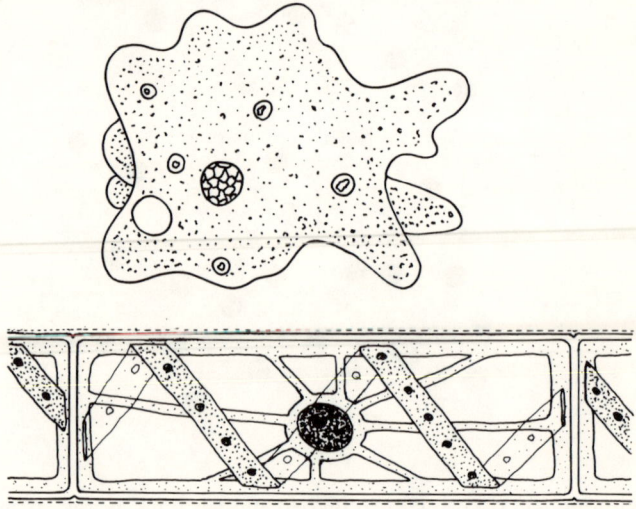

7 Movement in and out of cells: (iii) active uptake

[7.1] After digestion of food has occurred, the quite large molecules of sugar and amino acids are absorbed into cells and into the blood stream. Which of the following statements is UNTRUE?
A The molecules have to cross cell membranes, but are too large to pass through pores in the membrane.
B Energy is used in the process of absorption.
C It is possible for cells to select the substances absorbed.
D Movement of food molecules into cells occurs by diffusion.

[7.2] The plant roots are the site of uptake of mineral salts and ions from the soil. Which of the following statements is TRUE?
A Salts and ions are carried in passively with the water molecules entering by diffusion.

B Salts and ions diffuse into root cells from a high concentration in the soil to low concentration in the roots.
C Salts and ions are actively absorbed into the cells of the roots using energy released by respiration.
D Salts and ions are absorbed by osmosis.

8 Cells, tissues and organs; division of labour between cells

8.1 Tissues and organs are both made of cells. By means of brief definitions explain the difference between a *tissue* and an *organ*.

8.2 What does the term 'division of labour' mean when applied to living cells?

8.3 Name two plant tissues and two animal tissues with special functions, and state what is the special function of each.

8.4 For a named unicellular organism give two examples of division of labour in the cytoplasm of the cell.

8.5 The diagram below shows part of the body wall of a multicellular animal of the type having two layers of cells separated by a layer of jelly.

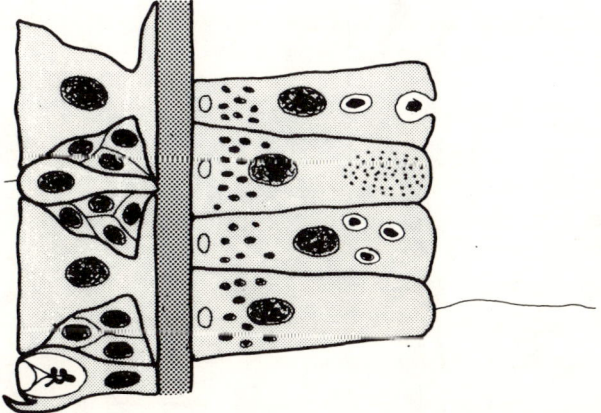

(a) Name one specific animal belonging to this group.
(b) Draw and label two cells of the inner layer and three cells of the outer layer to identify their special structure associated with their particular function.

12 Flowering plant, external structure

8.6 Draw and label two specialized cells each from
(a) a flowering plant, and
(b) a mammal.
For what particular task are these cells adapted?

9 Flowering plant, external structure

9.1 Using only the terms given below, make lists of the correct names of ten structures of the twig and of the herbaceous plant indicated in the drawing.

terminal bud, lateral bud, leaf scar, opposite leaf arrangement, spirally-arranged leaves in rosette form, leaf stalk (petiole), leaf blade (lamina), stem, bark, lenticel, ring scar, one-years' growth, lateral stem, fruit, inflorescence, tap root, lateral root.

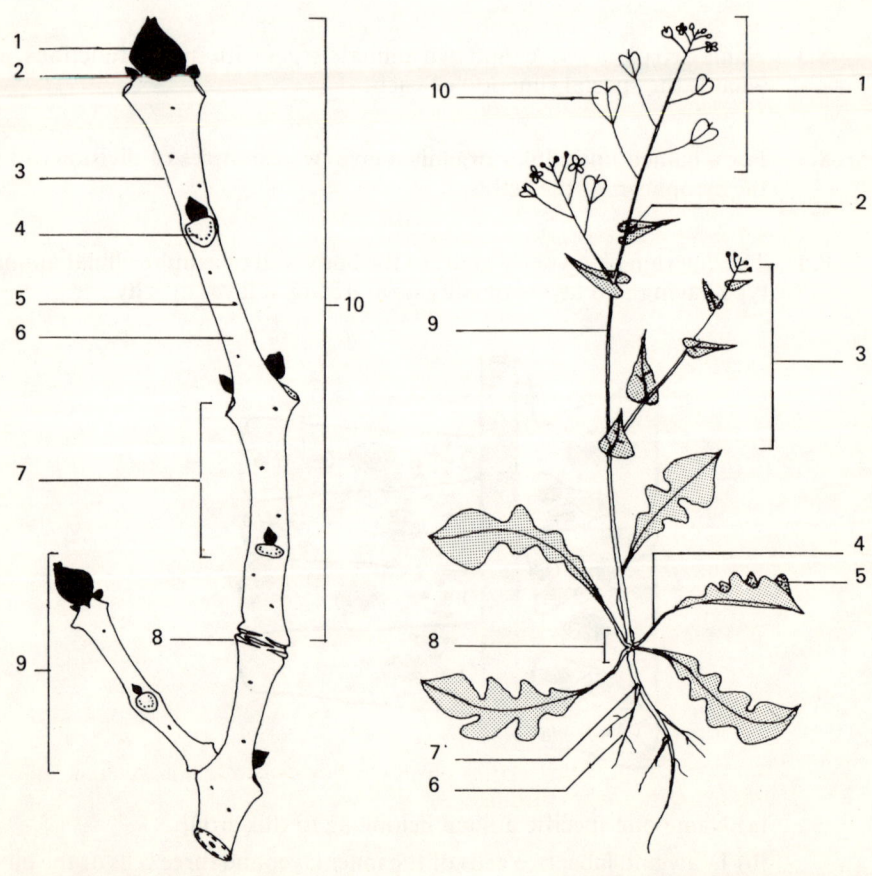

Ash twig in winter   **Shepherd's Purse plant**

9.2 Plant material of very diverse botanical origin is eaten as fruit and vegetable. Draw a simplified grid like the one below (using, just the numbers), then select an example (or examples) of each type from the list on the right and put the appropriate letter (or letters) in each empty box.

1 fruit eaten as vegetable	
2 fruit eaten as fruit	
3 leaf stalk as vegetable	
4 leaf stalk as 'fruit'	
5 inflorescence as vegetable	
6 inflorescence as fruit	
7 bud eaten as vegetable	
8 young stem eaten as vegetable	
9 whole leaf as vegetable	
10 underground stem as vegetable	
11 underground tap-root as vegetable	
12 seed as vegetable	
13 false fruit (receptacle and fruit grown together) as fruit	
14 sterile fruit (not containing seeds) as fruit	
15 fungal fruiting body producing spores eaten as vegetable	

A broccoli
B mushroom
C banana
D orange
E strawberry
F radish
G tomato
H turnip
I pea
J broad bean
K runner bean
O onion
P cucumber
Q carrot
R potato
S asparagus
T spinach
U Brussels sprout
V pineapple
W cauliflower
X celery
Y rhubarb
Z plum

10 Anatomy of stem, leaf and root

10.1 How does the arrangement of tissues in a herbaceous stem make it suitable for supporting branches and leaves?

10.2 How does the structure of a root make it suitable for growth in the soil and anchorage of the stem?

14 Anatomy of stem, leaf and root

10.3 Examine the drawing of sections through a stem and a root, and list the labels to the structures as indicated.

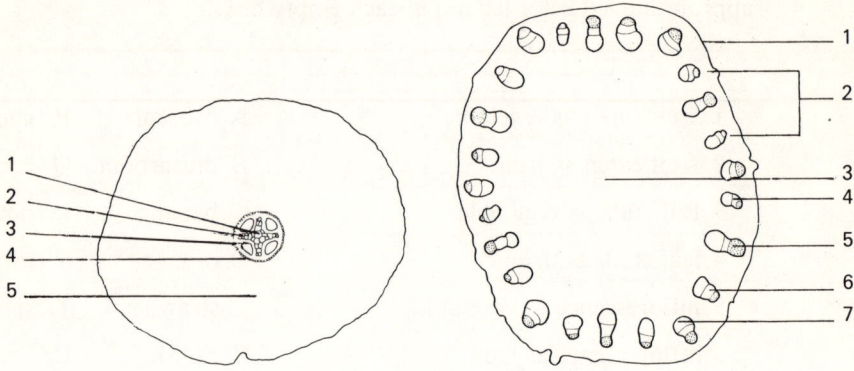

10.4 Make a list of the labels to the structures indicated in the drawing of a cross section of part of a leaf blade.

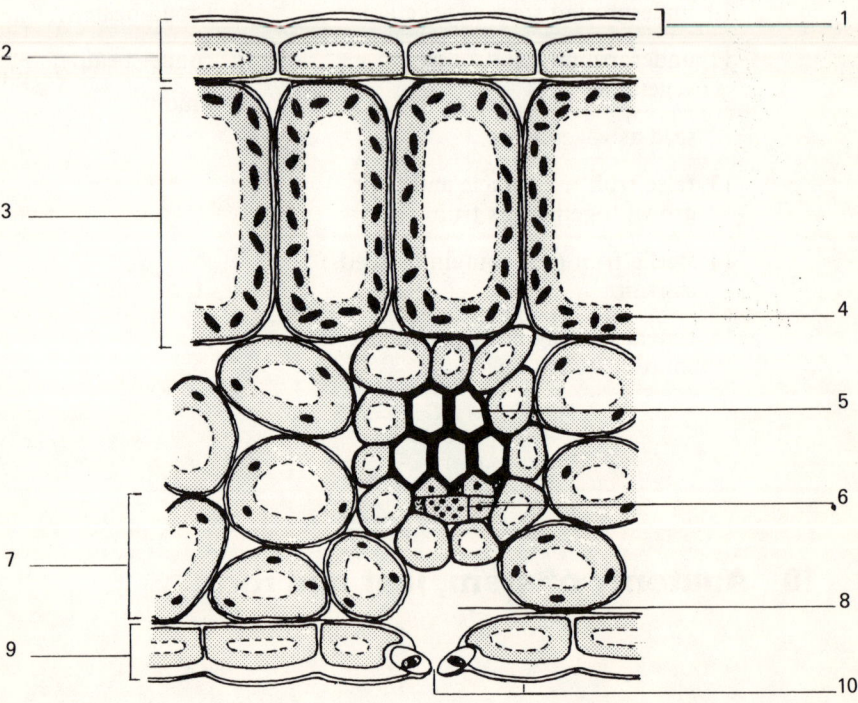

10.5 (a) State two functions that a green leaf with the structure shown would perform.

(b) State briefly how the structure of the leaf facilitates one of these functions.

11 Skeletons

11.1 Living things hold their bodies in a particular position in a variety of different ways. Copy the grid below and complete it by selecting the type of support typically adopted by each of the following organisms and inserting the appropriate letter in each box.

housefly	
earthworm	
blackbird	
shepherd's purse seedling	
horsechestnut tree	

A Fluid pressure acting against cellulose cell walls.

B Chitinous exoskeleton moved at joints by muscles.

C Bony endoskeleton moved at joints by muscles.

D Thickened cell walls strengthened with lignin.

E A hard shell strengthened with calcium carbonate.

F Fluid pressure acting against longitudinally and circularly arranged muscles.

11.2 The diagram below is of part of a limb of an insect seen in section.

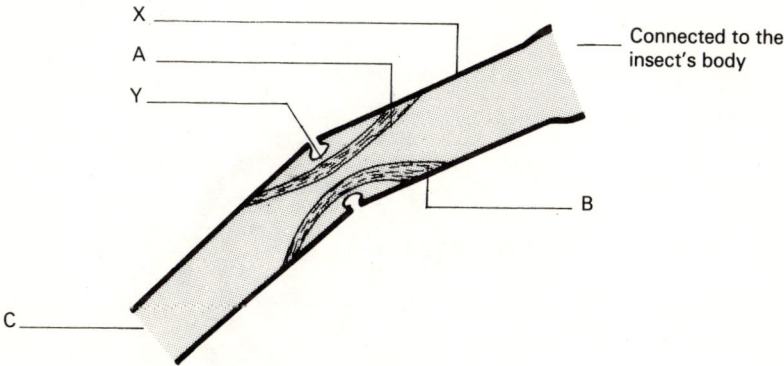

(a) When muscle A contracts what happens to:
  (i) the muscle B
  (ii) the limb at C?

(b) What is the important difference in the construction of the limb wall at X compared with Y?

(c) The interior of the limb contains muscles. Name one other important tissue that also occurs within this limb.

11.3 In the simplified drawing of the skeleton of the rabbit list the labels for the structures indicated as precisely as you are able.

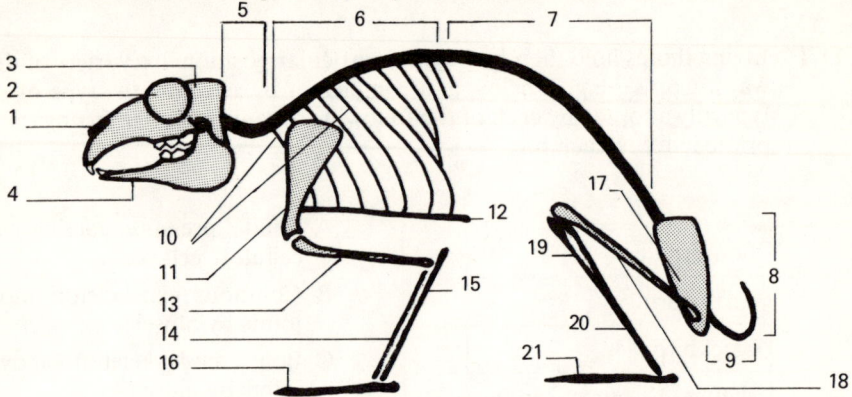

Simplified drawing of the skeleton of the rabbit

[11.4] The vertebrate limb is seen as a modification of an ancestral pentadactyl limb. What does 'pentadactyl' mean?

[11.5] What is the key structural difference between the fore limb of man and the fore limb of **(a)** a bat, **(b)** a cow, and **(c)** a whale?

11.6 Below is a diagram of a ball and socket joint as seen in section. Copy the diagram and label the structures indicated.

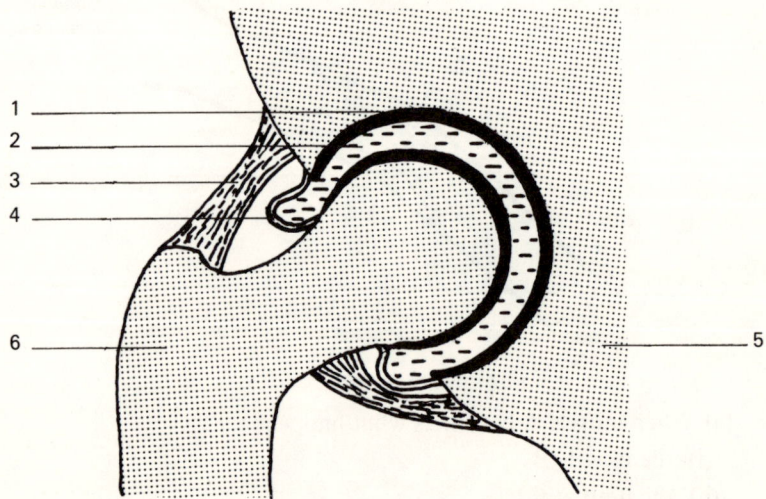

11.7 Certain parts of a mammal's skeleton, together with their associated muscles, act as a series of levers permitting movement. State TWO additional functions of parts of the mammalian skeleton.

11.8 Precisely where are the following to be found in the human skeleton?
  (a) a ball and socket joint
  (b) a neural arch
  (c) a tarsal
  (d) a hinge joint
  (e) a gliding joint
  (f) a centrum
  (g) ONE example of bones, muscles and joints forming a series of levers
    (i) with the 'load' central
    (ii) with the fulcrum central
    (iii) with the 'effort' central.

[11.9] Below is a diagram of the rabbit hind-limb in the crouched position. When the animal leaps which muscles (A, B, C, D, or E?) contract.
Sketch the bones and muscles when the limb is fully extended.

12 Teeth

12.1 Reptiles and amphibians swallow food whole, as quickly as possible, but in mammals digestion usually starts in the mouth where food can be held, and where it is cut up and chewed. Is this because only mammals have evolved:

  A four different types of teeth for breaking up solid food, or
  B a muscular tongue to move the food along to the back of the mouth, or
  C a nasal passage partly separated from the mouth by a palate, thus allowing breathing during chewing, or
  D an epiglottis involved in directing chewed food down the oesophagus?

18   Teeth

12.2 (a) Make a list of the labels to the structures numbered 1–6 in the diagram of a section through a tooth.

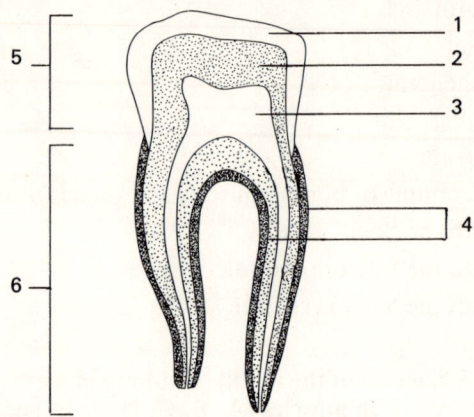

(b) What is the adaptation of 1 to its function?

(c) What is the difference in structure between parts 2 and 3?

12.3 How do the molar teeth of dogs, and sheep differ? For your answer sketch and label the working surface of the teeth.

12.4 Copy the table and complete it by stating the specialized role of incisors, canines and premolars in the dentition of the animals named.

	INCISORS	CANINES	PREMOLARS
(a) a typical herbivore, e.g. a cow			
(b) a typical carnivore, e.g. a dog			

12.5 (a) What does the term 'omnivore' mean?

(b) Name an animal that is omnivorous.

(c) What feature of the dentition is characteristic of an omnivore?

12.6 Explain fully the difference between:

(a) 'open' and 'closed' teeth

(b) 'carnassial' and 'canine' teeth.

12.7 (a) Why should we avoid excessive sweet sucking?

(b) Why do dentists have to make fewer fillings in childrens' teeth in areas of the world where fluoride occurs naturally in water?

13 Photosynthesis

13.1 Where did the carbon atoms in the starch formed in green leaf cells in the light come from:

A chlorophyll pigments in the chloroplasts
B carbon dioxide in the air
C ATP from mitochondria
D mineral salts absorbed from the soil?

13.2 The equation
$$6CO_2 + 6H_2O \longrightarrow C_6H_{12}C_6 + 6O_2$$
is too simple to represent the formation of sugar by photosynthesis. Rewrite the equation to include additional relevant information.

13.3 A potted plant with variegated leaves was left in total darkness for 48 hours. Then one leaf, still attached to the plant, had an opaque foil with stencil shape cut in it, attached as shown. After six hours exposure to sunlight the leaf was removed from the plant and tested for starch.

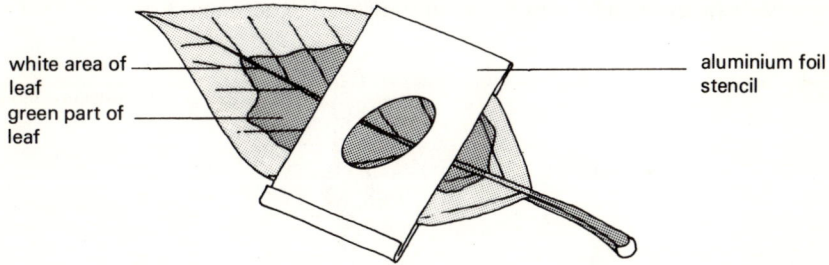

white area of leaf
green part of leaf
aluminium foil stencil

(a) Copy the table (leaving plenty of room in the boxes for your answers) and complete it by stating the four steps, in their correct order, that you would take to test the detached leaf for starch. Give a reason for each step.

STEP	REASON
1	
2	
3	
4	

(b) Not all the sugar formed in the green leaf in the light is converted into starch. State one other possible fate of sugar molecules formed in photosynthesis.

(c) (i) Why was the plant kept in darkness before the experiment was started?
   (ii) What additional test could have been wisely added to the experiment at the end of the dark period?

(d) Copy the diagram of the leaf and then state the colours of different areas after the starch test was completed.

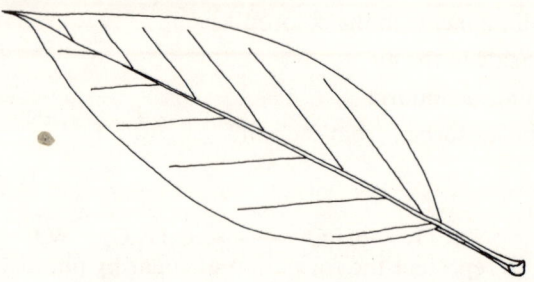

(e) What conclusions can you draw from this experiment?

(f) Why was it unnecessary to also detach and test a control leaf after the period of exposure to light?

13.4 The diagram represents a photosynthesis experiment which failed to give a conclusive result. What FOUR changes would be necessary to allow you to draw significant conclusions from an improved experiment?

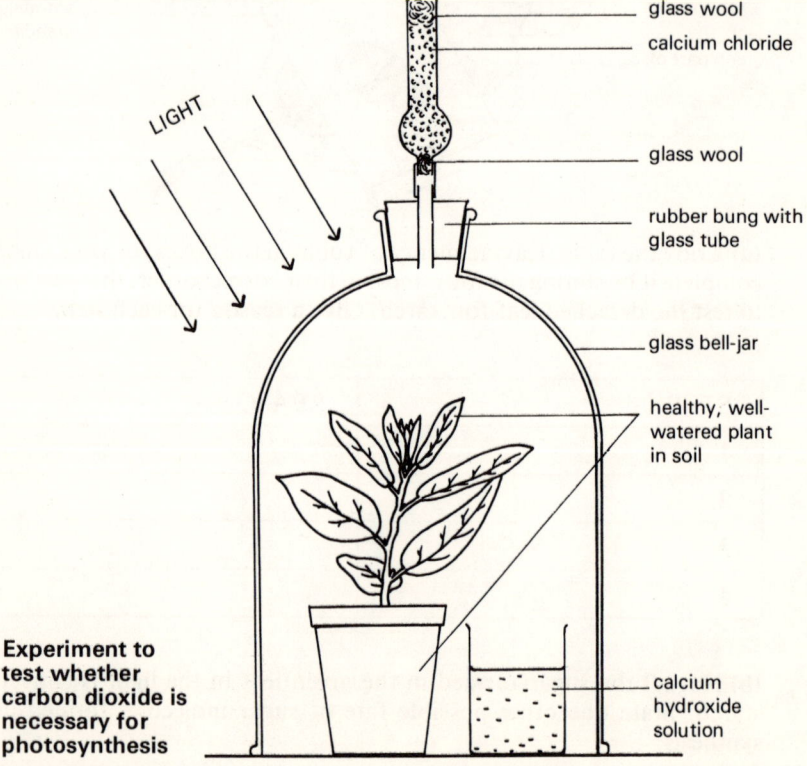

Experiment to test whether carbon dioxide is necessary for photosynthesis

13.5 What precisely is the value of photosynthesis to **(a)** a green plant, and **(b)** all living animals?

13.6 If radioactive carbon dioxide is made available to a green leaf in the light, we can obtain extra proof that during photosynthesis sugar and starch are built up. Which of the following statements is *untrue*?

 A Radioactive carbon dioxide gets into the leaf by the same pathway as unlabelled carbon dioxide.
 B Radioactivity can be detected in a leaf by subsequently pressing a detached leaf against photographic film in the dark.
 C Film exposed to radioactivity in the dark will show a dark image of the radioactive area in the leaf when the film is developed.
 D With time the radioactivity in a living leaf will also appear in many sugars, in amino acids, in proteins, and in new cell walls.
 E In this experiment a plant must first be destarched if newly formed, radioactive starch is to be detected at the end of the experiment.

14 Translocation and transpiration

14.1 By means of brief but precise definitions show the difference between *translocation* and *transpiration*.

14.2 What are the immediate sources of energy for movement of substances in **(a)** translocation, and **(b)** transpiration?

14.3 How would you most simply demonstrate that water *vapour* is lost from a leafy shoot?

14.4 Below is a drawing of some cells from the lower surface of a leaf, seen in surface view.

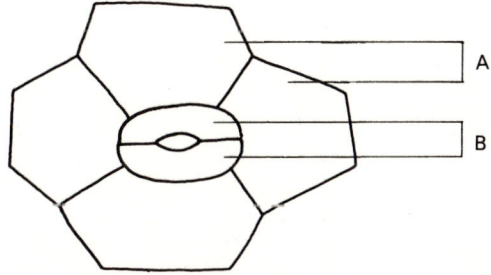

(a) State THREE differences between cells of type A and of type B.
(b) State two conditions usually necessary for the opening of the pore between cells B.

14.5 The following apparatus is called a *potometer*.

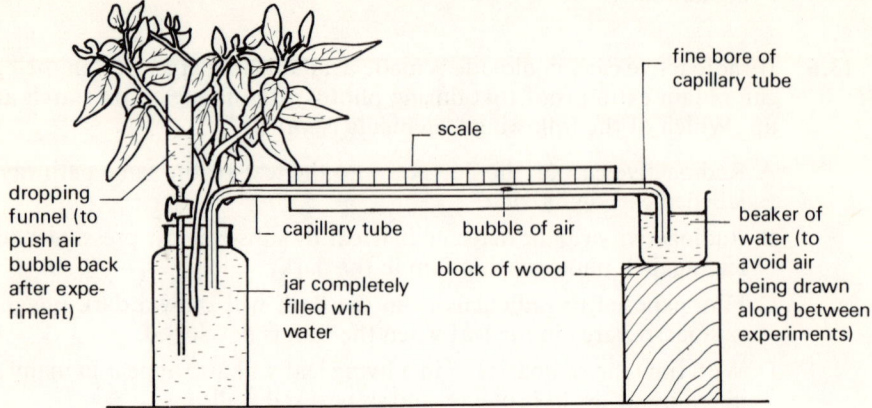

(a) Does the potometer measure water loss or water uptake by a leafy shoot?

(b) What precautions would you need to take in assembling the main jar with the leafy shoot?

(c) How would you take a reading with this apparatus as shown?

(d) How is the bubble returned from the left-hand side to the right-hand side of the scale?

(e) State two environmental conditions around the shoot that would slow transpiration.

(f) State two environmental conditions that would increase transpiration.

(g) What modification to the experiment would you add to confirm that most water vapour loss was occurring from the lower surface of the leaves of the plant under test?

[14.6] When the bark of a tree is ringed all around the stem, near the base, the tree eventually dies, but before this the bark above the ring swells up whereas that below shrinks quickly. What is your explanation for this?

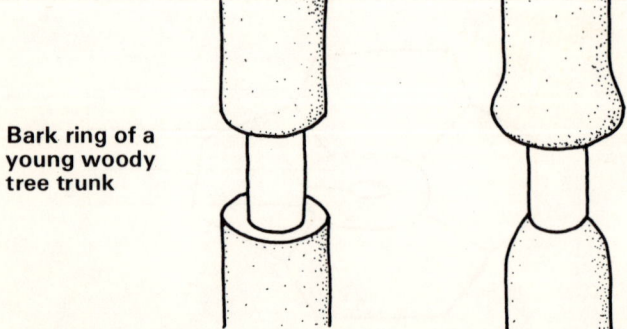

Bark ring of a young woody tree trunk

[14.7] In the experiment illustrated opposite, a jacket was assembled around part of the lower stem of the experimental plant so that steam could be passed over the stem in a narrow region.

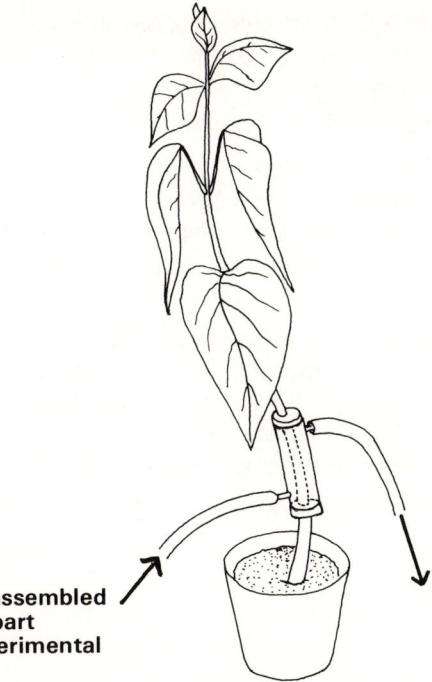

Steam jacket assembled around lower part of stem of experimental plant

It was found after the steam treatment that the stem did not wilt and the leaves remained turgid. However sugar and amino acids no longer reached the root cells. What is your explanation for this?

14.8 When a leafy shoot is freshly cut and stood in a weak solution of red dye for several hours, what would you expect to observe in thin transverse sections of the leaf stalks of large upper leaves when examined under the microscope?

14.9 Draw two large, fully labelled diagrams with one cell unit each, of the vascular tissue involved in **(a)** water movement and **(b)** sugar movement in plants, as seen in L.S.

15 Mineral nutrition

15.1 Which important element, found in all organisms, is not normally obtained from the soil?

15.2 **(a)** What do you understand by the term 'trace element'?
(b) List THREE trace elements.

15.3 (a) In each of the following cases, state ONE mineral element (obtained in food) which is particularly required by mammals for:
  (i) building skeletons
  (ii) making haemoglobin
  (iii) energy transfer reactions.

[(b)] For the three mineral elements mentioned in your answer to (a) above, state to what use a healthy flowering plant puts these elements.

[(c)] From where does a flowering plant normally obtain these elements?

15.4 If a plant is cultured with its roots in a dilute solution of all essential elements, its growth is healthy. If other plants of the same species are grown in a medium deficient in nitrogen (as nitrate ions, for example) and magnesium, the plants are pale yellow with weak, thin stems.
(a) What is the term for this condition?
(b) To what uses are (i) nitrogen, and (ii) magnesium put in the healthy plant?

16 Soil

16.1 (a) A sample of soil is added to water in a clear glass bottle. After corking, the bottle is shaken vigorously and then stood upright. Make a drawing to show where you would expect to find various parts of the soil. Label the drawing fully.

(b) In collecting and comparing two different soils by this method, what precautions would you take to ensure reasonable accuracy?

(c) What (visible) differences would you expect if clay and sandy soils are treated in this way?

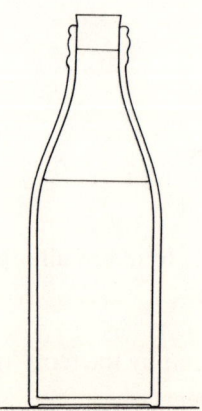

16.2 What type of soil (e.g. sandy, clay, etc.) is often associated with natural growth of a preponderance of: **(a)** oak, hawthorn and buttercup, **(b)** beech and bee orchid, **(c)** coniferous trees, gorse and heather?

16.3 Below is a magnified view of a loam soil sample showing soil crumbs.

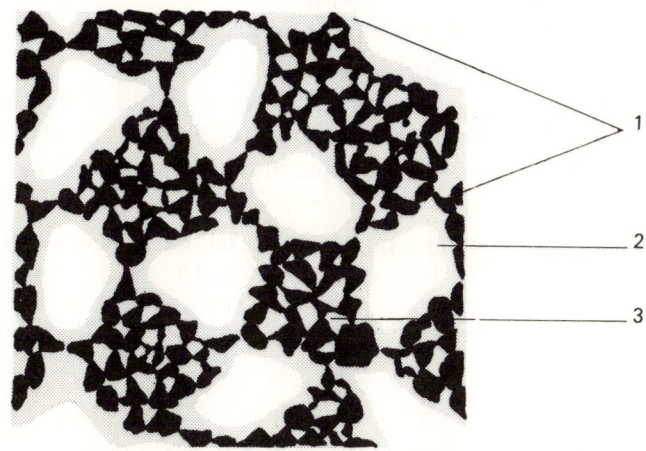

(a) Make a list of the labels to the features numbered 1–3.

(b) What is the name of the scarcely visible yet sticky coating around mineral particles that glues them into crumbs, and from what is it formed?

(c) Which component of the soil is a source of nitrate ions for plants?

(d) How does loam soil differ from clay soil in composition?

16.4 You are required to outline how you would use the apparatus in the diagram to compare the rates of drainage of two contrasting soils by answering the following questions.

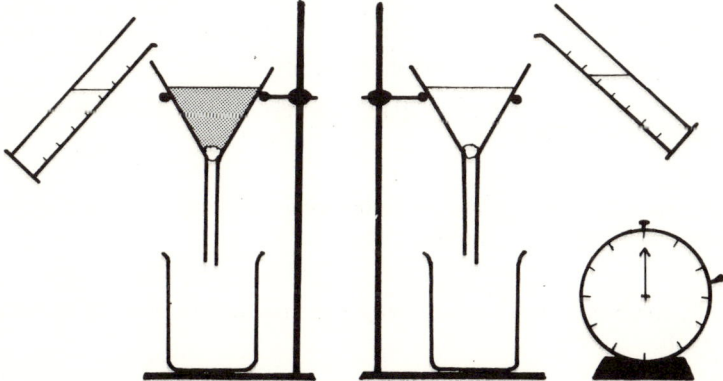

(a) Would you arrange for the water content of the soil samples at the start of the experiment to be (i) dry, (ii) slightly damp, or (iii) at field capacity (as much water as the soil can hold against gravity)? Why?

(b) How would you conduct the experiment starting with a measured volume of tap water in each measuring cylinder?

(c) Why do some soils drain more readily than others?

(d) What result would you anticipate if soil A was pure sand and soil B was clay?

(e) State TWO advantages for plant growth that result from good soil drainage.

(f) State TWO disadvantages for plant growth that result from good drainage.

16.5 **(a)** Give ONE reason for the improvement in the tilth of a heavy clay soil in spring, following ploughing (or rough digging) in the previous autumn.

(b) Explain how the addition of lime to a clay soil may improve plant yield.

16.6 A soil sample was brought into the laboratory and exactly 50 g were spread out in shallow trays in an oven at 100°C. The sample was weighed after cooling at 3 days and 5 days. The weights were:

initial sample	50.0 g
after 3 days	43.0 g
after 5 days	43.0 g.

(a) What change occurred to the soil in the oven?

The sample was then transferred to a heat-proof crucible and very strongly heated by Bunsen flame for one hour. It was then allowed to cool.

(b) What change to the soil composition would occur during heating?

(c) What change in the colour of the soil sample would occur during heating? When cooled the weight of the soil sample was found to be 38.0 g.

(d) What percentage of the original soil sample was (i) water, and (ii) organic matter or humus?

[(e)] If carbonates were present in the soil, how would this affect your conclusion in (d) above?

16.7 In the growth of plant crops what major steps does the farmer take to:

(a) maintain the humus content of the soil

(b) deliver nitrates, potash, and phosphates to a cash crop early in its growth to improve the yield?

16.8 State THREE advantages to the farmer or gardener of rotating the crops that are grown on land over a number of years.

16.9 State concisely TWO reasons why the presence of soil air is vital for plant growth.

16.10 Given a stout metal tube that has been driven into the soil with minimum disturbance, and now contains a known volume of soil sample, how would you find the air content of the soil using simple school laboratory apparatus?

Soil 27

16.11 An experiment to test for the presence of living organisms in soil is carried out as follows. Two small quantities of milk are simmered for 10 minutes as shown, then the milk is allowed to cool. One soil sample is heated STRONGLY in a crucible. A second soil sample is not heated.

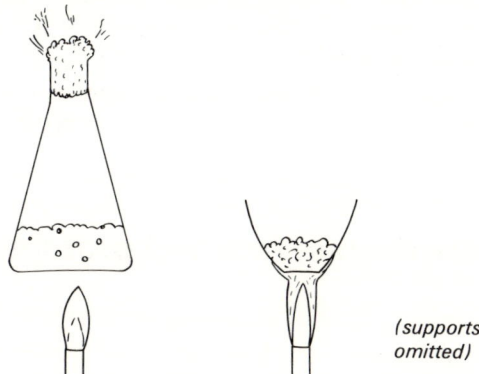

(supports omitted)

The treated soil is cooled and added to one lot of milk. Untreated soil is added to the second lot of milk. The milk is inspected daily.

(a) Why is milk used?

(b) Why is only a small sample of milk used?

(c) Why is a cotton-wool plug used?

(d) Why is the milk simmered for several minutes?

(e) Why is the milk cooled before adding the soil samples?

(f) Why is one lot of soil heated strongly?

(g) What visible differences would you expect to find in the two lots of milk after a day or two?

(h) If no difference developed in the two lots of milk, what conclusions may be drawn?

[16.12] Below is drawn the surface view of three sealed Petri dishes in which diluted washings from soil samples have been added to sterile Dox's Agar medium (suitable for culturing soil micro-organisms). Dish A was inoculated from garden loam soil, dish B was inoculated from acidic heathland soil, and dish C was inoculated with a heat-sterilized soil sample.

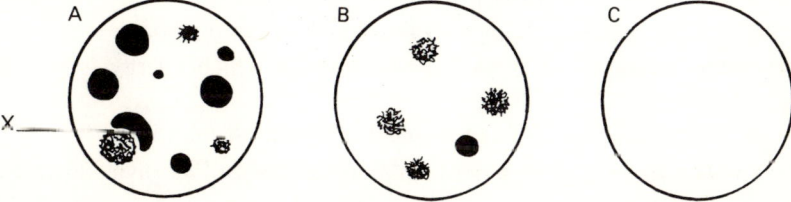

(a) Some colonies are smooth and slimy-looking, others are fluffy and powdery. Which of these two types of colony is made of bacteria?

(b) What might we suspect about the proportions of fungi to bacteria in an acid soil by comparing dish B with A?

(c) What does the control dish help us to establish about the origin of the micro-organisms growing on dishes A and B?

(d) Why is it important not to open these Petri dishes at the end of the experiment in order to inspect the colonies closely?

(e) There appears to be abnormal growth at X in dish A. What may have happened at this point?

(f) Micro-organisms of the soil play an important part in the creation of humus in soil. What is humus, and from what is it produced?

17 Carbohydrates, fats and proteins as foods

17.1 What constituents of food provide: (a) energy, (b) roughage, and (c) nitrogen?

17.2 What constituent of food is present if a positive result occurs when testing with the following:

(a) Benedict's (or Fehling's) solution (boiled)

(b) Millon's reagent (boiled)

(c) iodine solution

(d) excess of sodium hydroxide solution plus a trace of copper sulphate solution?

17.3 If too much food is regularly eaten by a mammal, where in its body is reserve food usually stored?

17.4 Select one different plant in each case which deposits food material in the following parts: (a) tap root, (b) root tuber, (c) stem tuber, (d) underground stem, (e) bud, (f) inflorescence, (g) receptacle, (h) cotyledon.

17.5 (a) Which of the following definitions of *metabolism* is correct?

A The removal of waste products from the body.
B All the chemical changes of life that occur in the body.
C The sequence of chemical reactions in which energy is released from glucose.
D The production of food by plants containing chlorophyll.
E The interrelationship between an organism and its environment.

(b) For basic metabolism only, during 24 hours, a man requires approximately 7500 kJ. State the approximate requirements in kJ for one day for:

(i) a man working in an office,

(ii) a working coalman,

(iii) a boy aged 15–19 years.

17.6 (a) How do the energy values of carbohydrates, fats, and proteins compare with one another?

(b) If amino acids are respired by a mammal what change is first made to them in the liver?

17.7 (a) What is the value of carbohydrates in our food?

(b) What happens in the body to carbohydrates which are eaten in excess?

(c) Name a common vegetable containing sugar.

(d) Which chemical elements are present in carbohydrates?

(e) List the following carbohydrates in decreasing order of solubility in water:

starch, glucose, cellulose, sucrose.

17.8 Write a chemical equation representing the formation of cane sugar from simple sugars.

17.9 (a) What is the name of the repeating unit from which the long unbranched cellulose molecule is made up?

(b) What food source regularly eaten by many mammals contains cellulose?

(c) Name one group of organisms able to digest cellulose.

17.10 How do fats (or oils) differ in composition from carbohydrates?

17.11 (a) Describe how you would test for fat in food, and describe the appearance of a positive result.

(b) Which of the following foods would give a positive result to a fat test:

cheese, white flour, brown flour, pork meat, skimmed milk?

17.12 State two differences in chemical composition between proteins and carbohydrates.

17.13 (a) What is a 'polypeptide'?

(b) Which part of a mammal's body contains little protein?

(c) Why are proteins a necessary part of our diet?

(d) Which items in a vegetarian's diet supply protein? Name three major sources.

18 Balanced diet; water, vitamins, minerals, roughage

18.1 Many items of food contain carbohydrates, fats and proteins. What other groups of chemical compounds form essential constituents of our food?

18.2 Why is water such a vital ingredient of a healthy diet?

18.3 What change in food value may occur when fresh fruit, vegetables and milk are cooked?

18.4 State three uses to which calcium is put in the human body.

18.5 Why are vitamins required in only minute amounts on a regular basis?

18.6 (a) Which disease may develop if polished rice alone is eaten?
(b) What parts of the rice fruit are removed in 'polishing'?
(c) Which important items of diet are removed in rice 'polishing'?

18.7 (a) Which one vitamin is particularly present in potatoes, oranges, black-currants and Brussels sprouts?
(b) Which deficiency disease results in humans deprived of this vitamin?

18.8 What difference in solubility permits some vitamins to be stored in our bodies, others not?

18.9 What may be lacking in the diet of a person suffering from: (a) rickets, (b) anaemia, (c) night blindness, (d) goitre?

18.10 Name an organism which requires no intake of vitamins.

19 Enzymes

19.1 (a) What do you understand by the term *catalyst*?
(b) State TWO differences between enzymes and inorganic catalysts.

19.2 The effect of boiling an enzyme may be tested in a starch-digestion experiment.
(a) Which enzyme would you use?

(b) For how long would you boil the enzyme?

(c) How would you prepare the starch?

(d) What starch-enzyme mixtures would you prepare to test the effect of boiling the enzyme?

(e) Name any test(s) performed at the beginning of the experiment.

(f) How do you know when the experiment is finished?

(g) Which further tests are performed at the end of the experiment?

(h) State what result would indicate that boiling affects enzymes.

19.3 Which of the following statements about enzymes are CORRECT?

A Enzymes are produced in cells from proteins.
B Enzymes are only active inside living cells.
C A small quantity of enzyme is effective in any reaction it catalyses.
D Enzymes are entirely destroyed in the reactions they catalyse.
E Enzymes are involved in most processes of cells, not only in the digestion of food.
F Enzymes are living substances that are killed by heat and by extremes of acidity and alkalinity.

19.4 For the statements that are incorrect in 19.3 above rewrite them, correcting the errors they contain.

[19.5] Why does gelatin jelly liquefy when certain bacteria grow on it, and yet agar jelly does not?

19.6 Five test-tubes labelled A, B, C, D and E, each containing 5 cm^3 of cloudy egg white suspension, were stood in a water bath at 37°C. To the test-tubes the following additions were made:

Tube A   1 cm^3 of 1% pepsin solution,

Tube B   1 cm^3 distilled water with 5 drops of dilute hydrochloric acid,

Tube C   1 cm^3 of 1% pepsin solution with 5 drops of dilute hydrochloric acid,

Tube D   1 cm^3 of 1% pepsin solution that had previously been boiled and cooled, with 5 drops of dilute hydrochloric acid,

Tube E   1 cm^3 of water.

After 10 minutes the tubes were withdrawn from the water bath and examined for differences in the cloudiness of the suspension, using tube E for the comparison. State what results you would anticipate, and give your reasons, listing them as follows:

Tube A   Result: Tube B   Result:
         Reason: etc.

Feeding and digestion

[19.7] What is autolysis?

19.8 If milk is kept in a warm place and not covered from dust it sours in a short time. Explain precisely why this is so.

[19.9] Germinating maize fruit from which part of the food store had been sliced away were placed on the surface of a starch/agar medium in a Petri dish. One of the grains was held in boiling water for 3 minutes before slicing.

After 24 hours the starch in zone L was converted to sugar. What three deductions can you make from this?

[19.10] (a) How would you test the effect of adding the salt of a heavy metal to an enzyme?

(b) What is the likely effect of Millon's reagent on an enzyme?

[19.11] Yeast utilizes sugars. Devise an experiment to test whether yeast sucrase (invertase) enzyme acts outside the yeast cells.

20 Feeding and digestion

20.1 Living organisms obtain food in a variety of ways. Copy the grid below and complete it by selecting the most appropriate description of feeding for each of the following organisms and inserting the appropriate letter in each box.

Organism	
Amoeba	
Hydra	
tapeworm	
housefly	
herring	
frog	
chaffinch	
rabbit	

A This is a parasite, and absorbs digested food molecules and water from its surroundings.
B Feeds on liquids or solids that quickly dissolve in salivary juices pumped out onto food. Liquid is then sucked back up through the proboscis pads.
C Feeds by stinging small water animals and pulling the stunned prey into the body cavity for digestion.
D Feeds on plankton strained from the water by gill rakers as a young animal, but adults also swallow small molluscs.
E Feeds on seeds and grains which are pecked up into a toothless mouth, swallowed whole, and ground up in a muscular gizzard.
F Feeds by flowing of cytoplasm around microscopic algae, bacteria and protozoa that live in the surrounding mud.
G Young feed in water, but adults catch worms, slugs, or flies often using their long sticky tongue.
H Bites off and grinds up plant material in their mouths, but once this is swallowed they also make use of bacteria to help in digestion of cellulose.

20.2 (a) Make a list of the labels to the structures numbered 1–16 in the diagram of the alimentary canal drawn.

(b) State THREE differences in the structure of the alimentary canals of the rabbit and man.

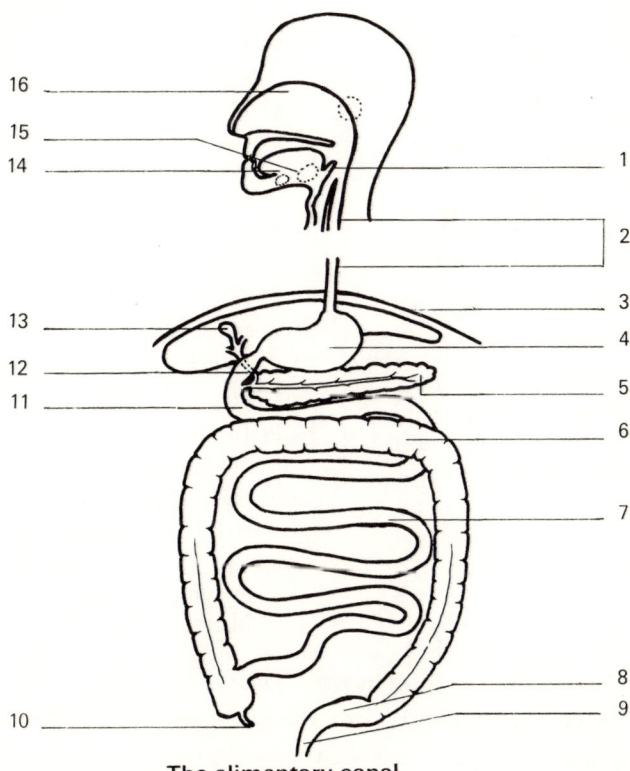

The alimentary canal

34 Feeding and digestion

[20.3] Bacteria play an important part in food digestion by herbivores. Copy the table and complete it to show similarities and differences in digestion of the rabbit and cow.

	RABBIT	COW
(a) The type of food that bacteria help to digest.		
(b) Site of this bacterial action.		
(c) Pathway taken by products of bacterial digestion from the site of digestion until absorbed.		

20.4 The grid below lists aspects of digestion in mammals. Draw a simplified grid, using just the numbers rather than the complete descriptions, and complete it by selecting the correct site or organ from the list A-J and inserting the appropriate letter in each box.

1	Tough meat cut into pieces by a dog.	
2	The food bolus is moved from mouth to stomach.	
3	The completion of the conversion of maltose to glucose.	
4	The commencement of fat digestion by the enzyme lipase.	
5	Protein digestion is commenced.	
6	Partly digested food is abruptly changed from an acid to an alkaline medium.	

A In the stomach with the aid of gastric juice.
B In the mouth by the aid of the enzyme salivary amylase (ptyalin).
C In the mouth by the action of the carnassial teeth.
D In the oesophagus by waves of contraction and the temporary relaxation of the sphincter muscle at entry to stomach.
E In the duodenum by the addition of bile from the gall bladder.
F In the mouth by the ripping action of incissor teeth.
G In the duodenum with the aid of enzymes from the pancreas.
H In the small intestine with the aid of enzymes there.
I By anti-peristalsis and relaxation of the pyloric sphincter muscle.
J In the appendix by the action of enzymes (cellulases) produced by bacteria.

20.5 For the digestion of food by man, give:
(a) THREE processes which occur in the buccal cavity (mouth)
(b) THREE processes which occur in the stomach

(c) THREE enzymes produced by the small intestine
(d) THREE products obtained from brown bread.

20.6 (a) Why is digestion an essential stage in feeding?
(b) Name TWO constituents of food which are *not* digested.

20.7 How would *you* test whether the digestion of a given protein takes place mainly in the stomach or in the small intestine?

20.8 (a) What changes in acidity (pH) occur during digestion of our food, and where do these changes occur?
(b) Would you expect (i) lactase and (ii) invertase to work faster in an acid or an alkaline medium? Give a reason.

20.9 State TWO consequences of the secretion of bile.

20.10 At what temperature would you expect salivary amylase (ptyalin) to work most efficiently and how would *you* test your answer?

20.11 What is absorbed by the bloodstream in the villi if a meal contains: **(a)** salted butter, **(b)** table sugar, **(c)** white of egg, **(d)** glucose (dextrose)?

20.12 Most grafts of 'foreign' tissue are liable to rejection by the body, but tissue from many sources can be eaten. Offer an explanation.

21 Absorption and assimilation

21.1 (a) State one gas, one liquid and one solid normally absorbed into the human body daily.
(b) In what physical state must these be in order to be absorbed?

21.2 What do you understand by the following terms:
(a) completely permeable
(b) selectively permeable
(c) 'active' uptake
(d) diffusion?

21.3 State **(a)** one similarity, and **(b)** one difference in oxygen uptake by (i) *Amoeba* and (ii) a human.

36 Absorption and assimilation

21.4 (a) How and where does carbon dioxide enter the cells of a green leaf during photosynthesis?

(b) Where does the absorption of food take place in the human body?

(c) State THREE common characteristics of efficient absorption surfaces.

21.5 Copy out and complete the following: 'Carbohydrates are transported through living organisms in the form of ....; proteins are transported in the form of ....; and fats (oils) in the form of ....'.

21.6 What is the main route of transport of sugar:

(a) in flowering plants from a palisade mesophyll cell to a storage site

(b) in mammals from the small intestine to the liver?

21.7 (a) A hundred healthy young plants are exposed to bright sunlight for six hours. Fifty are then put into a dark room at a temperature of 5°C and fifty are put into a dark room at a temperature of 20°C. Using a cork borer to sample portions of leaves, how would you test whether:

(i) some food is transported from mature leaves to young leaves,

(ii) the rate of movement of food from leaves varies with temperature?

(b) How would you determine the optimum (best) temperature for transport of food in these plants?

[21.8] State in outline the key steps of a method of investigating movement of food from leaves of a plant, using a radio-isotope, such as ^{14}C.

21.9 Draw and label the diagram of a villus and annotate it to show which products of digestion are absorbed by the vessels shown.

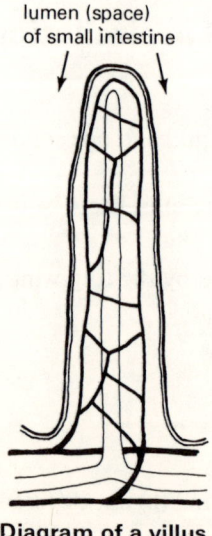

Diagram of a villus

21.10 For each of the following statements concerning the fate or role of the absorbed products of digestion in the mammal, state whether true or false.

(a) Much of the glucose will be respired in living cells.

(b) Fats are used in cell membranes or are oxidized to release much energy.

(c) Amino acids are absorbed into cells and reassembled to make proteins to be used in enzymes and in membranes.

(d) Fats are simple, oxygen-rich molecules which assist in metabolism generally.

(e) Excess amino acids are not stored in the body but are deaminated in the liver.

(f) Excess fats can be stored under the skin and in connective tissue near the kidney.

(g) Excess glucose is mostly stored as starch as a food reserve in the body.

(h) Excess amino acids are transferred to the kidney and converted to urea in the kidney tubule.

(i) Excess glucose initially is stored as glycogen in the liver, but subsequently additional glucose is converted to fat and stored elsewhere.

21.11 (a) State the three major ingredients of bile.

(b) Where is bile produced?

(c) Where is bile temporarily stored?

(d) For patients unable to produce bile what change in their diet is recommended to them?

21.12 Explain what is meant by the term 'threshold' level in relation to the regulation of sugar level by the liver.

21.13 Outline the steps involved in the metabolism by the liver of amino acids that are excess to body needs.

22 Blood and lymphatic systems

22.1 Blood is a red, syrupy fluid. If a sample of blood to which anti-clotting substance has been added is allowed to stand (or is centrifuged), the blood separates under gravity into three layers in the proportions shown overleaf:

38 Blood and lymphatic systems

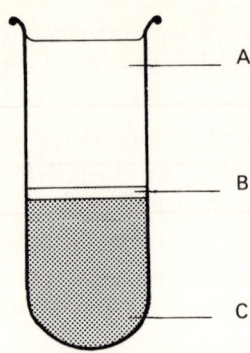

(a) Copy the grid and complete it by giving the name and content of each layer and stating the chief role or major task performed by each in the body.

Component	Name and contents	Chief role or task performed
A		
B		
C		

(b) What does *clotting of blood* mean?

(c) If a sample of blood is allowed to stand without addition of anti-clotting substance, into what components does the blood sample separate?

22.2 In conducting the microscope examination of a blood sample taken from your hand place the following stages in sequence:

A Stain with Leishman's stain and examine cells under the high-power or oil immersion lens.

B Pierce the skin with a sterilized lancet so that a drop of blood appears at the skin surface.

C Spread the blood evenly over the slide with the edge of a rectangular cover slip and quickly air-dry the smear.

D Touch a clean microscope slide on the drop of blood for examination.

E Using ethanol on cotton-wool, very carefully sterilize the skin at the tip of the thumb.

22.3 (a) Which of the following statements are CORRECT?

A Platelets are small fragments of cells that help the clotting process by stopping leakage of blood from a damaged blood vessel.

B Red cells are the most numerous of blood cells, contain haemoglobin, and are made and lose their nuclei in the marrow of bones.

C Plasma is a yellow-coloured liquid made of water containing dissolved chemicals which are food, waste-substances, salts, hormones, and dissolved gases.

D White cells move out of capillaries by squeezing between cells of the capillary wall to attack invading germs at the site of a wound.

E All vertebrates are warm-blooded and use their blood as a central-heating system that generates heat for the cold inner parts of their bodies.

F White cells are larger than red cells, have nuclei but no fixed shape, and are made in lymph glands and in the spleen.

(b) Rewrite any incorrect statement so that it is entirely correct.

22.4 There are three types of vessel in which blood passes around the body. In the drawing of cross-sections of these vessels below

(a) list the names of the three types A, B and C, and

(b) make a list of the names of the layers that make up the walls.

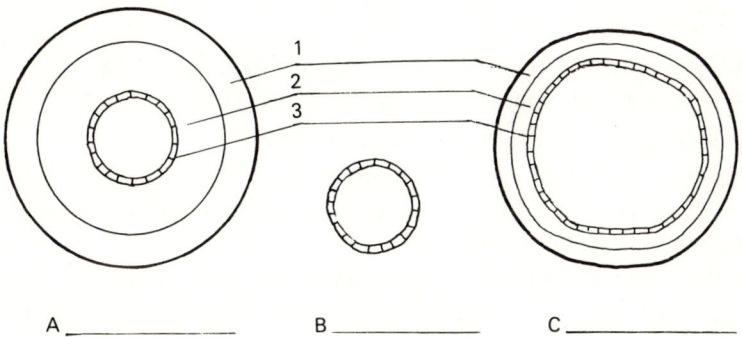

(c) What prevents the back-flow of blood in A and C?

22.5 Copy the diagram illustrating the structure of a capillary network, and annotate it to show:

(a) how the cells are supplied with oxygen and dissolved nutrients

(b) how cells lose excretory products

(c) the paths by which blood and lymph drain away.

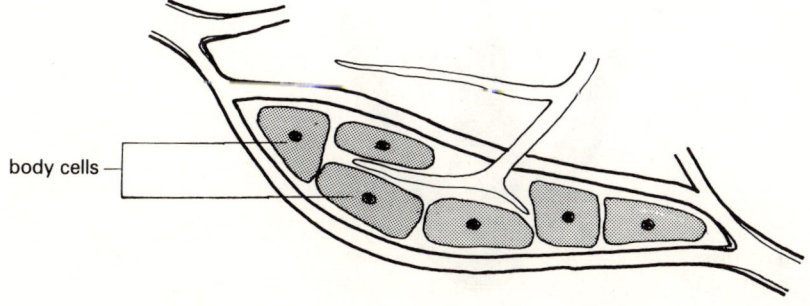

40 Blood and lymphatic systems

22.6 The drawing shows a view of a mammalian heart with some of the surrounding blood vessels.

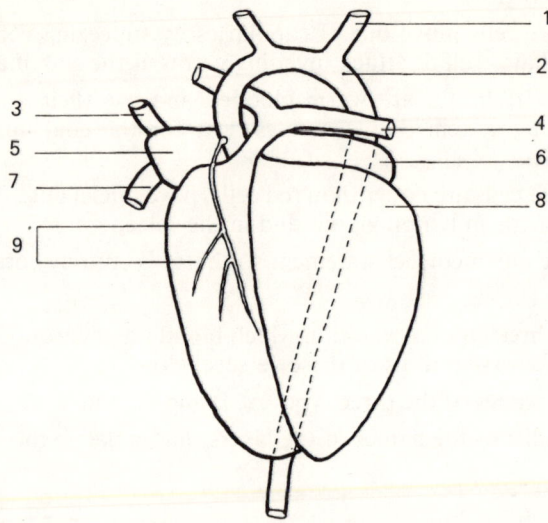

(a) List the names of the structures labelled 2, 4, 5, 7 and 8.
(b) Where would blood passing through 1 be moving towards?
(c) Where would blood in 3 be returning from?
(d) What tissue does the artery 9 supply?
(e) The veins joining 6 are not shown here, but from where in the body do veins run to empty blood into 6?
(f) What do you understand by the term 'double circulation'?
[(g)] Name a group of animals that have a single circulation and state how many chambers the heart contains.

22.7 The drawing shows the working of the heart of a mammal.

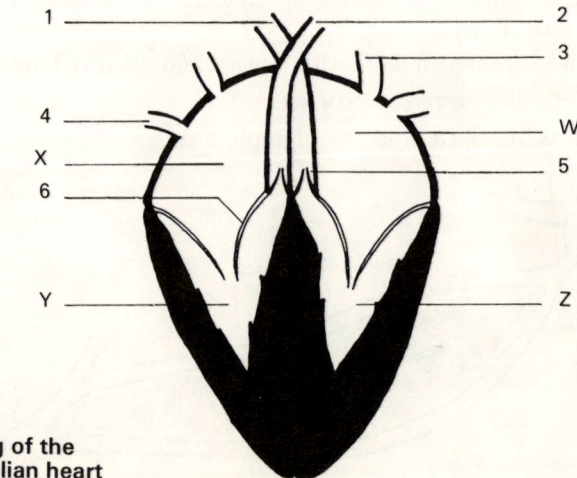

Working of the mammalian heart

(a) State whether blood normally flows *into* or *out of* the heart at 1, 2, 3, and 4.

(b) List the structures indicated by 1–6.

(c) Which of the chambers identified as W, X, Y and Z is the LEFT VENTRICLE and the RIGHT ATRIUM?

(d) What is the function of 5?

22.8 (a) Copy the table and complete it by naming the main artery and the main vein which serve the parts of the body listed in column one.

PART OF BODY	MAIN ARTERY	MAIN VEIN
head	....	....
arm	....	....
lungs	....	....
liver	....	....
kidney	....	....

(b) What is the name of the vessel that carries blood direct from the small intestine to the liver? How does this vein differ from the other veins of the body?

22.9 State TWO ways in which the heart responds to strenuous exercise.

22.10 (a) Give SIX functions of the blood system.

(b) (i) What is the general usefulness of having the pulse rate of a patient recorded?

(ii) Why can the pulse be felt only at certain points?

23 Respiration, aerobic and anaerobic; gaseous exchange

23.1 Make a table like the one below and list THREE differences between external respiration (gaseous exchange) and internal respiration (tissue respiration).

EXTERNAL RESPIRATION	INTERNAL RESPIRATION

23.2 Copy the two diagrams, then **(a)** insert arrows to indicate movement of gases during respiration, **(b)** label and annotate them to show any similarities in the external respiration of a flowering plant and a mammal.

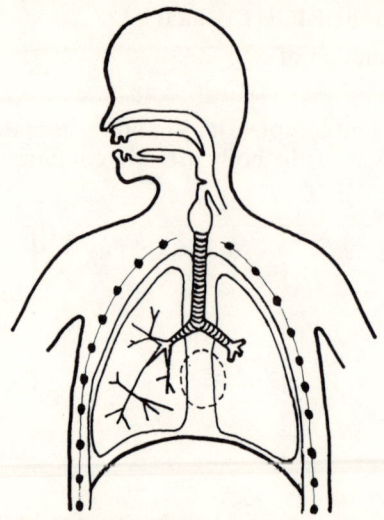

Thorax cut open to show the lungs

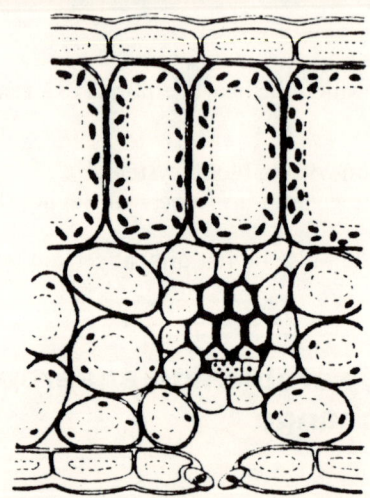

Section through a leaf blade

23.3 **(a)** What happens to oxygen before it can enter living cells?

(b) What useful process follows the entry of oxygen into active living cells? Write an equation in words or formulae for this process.

(c) Copy and complete the following equations:

ADP + phosphate +   ⟶ ATP
ATP ⟶ ADP +   +

(d) Give FIVE uses of energy made by both plants and animals.

(e) State FIVE examples of energy expenditure by mammals, not found in flowering plants.

23.4 Examine the apparatus shown below.

(a) Why is air bubbled through the solution in A?

(b) Name another substance which could be used instead of sodium hydroxide.

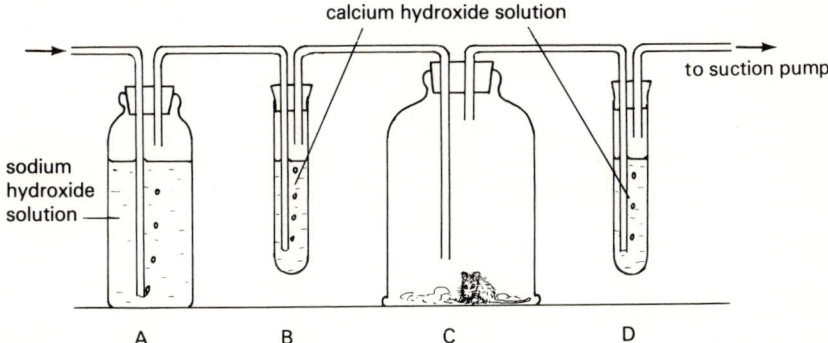

(c) State with a reason what occurs when carbon dioxide bubbles through calcium hydroxide (or bicarbonate indicator).

(d) What does the experiment test?

(e) How soon should the experiment be stopped?

(f) Give a modification which is necessary in order to use the apparatus for a flowering plant.

(g) Could a valid conclusion be drawn if the apparatus is used without part A? Give reasons.

23.5 (a) What is the approximate composition of air breathed in? Give your answer as follows:
    Oxygen = %,   carbon dioxide = %,   nitrogen, etc. = %

(b) State which gas in (a) may have (i) increased in percentage (ii) decreased in percentage or (iii) not changed, in the air subsequently breathed out.

(c) Draw a diagram of an apparatus suitable for contrasting the amounts of carbon dioxide present in air breathed in and air breathed out.

(d) Why does an athlete pant after running a race?

(e) What is 'tidal air' (in mammals)?

23.6 Where does exchange of gases take place in: (a) a fish, (b) a frog, (c) a bird, (d) an earthworm, (e) an insect?

23.7 In the experiment illustrated overleaf the bell jar is lowered as far as possible before the rubber tubing connecting the air inside and outside the bell jar is removed.

(a) What visible change would you expect to occur after some hours?

44 Respiration, aerobic and anaerobic; gaseous exchange

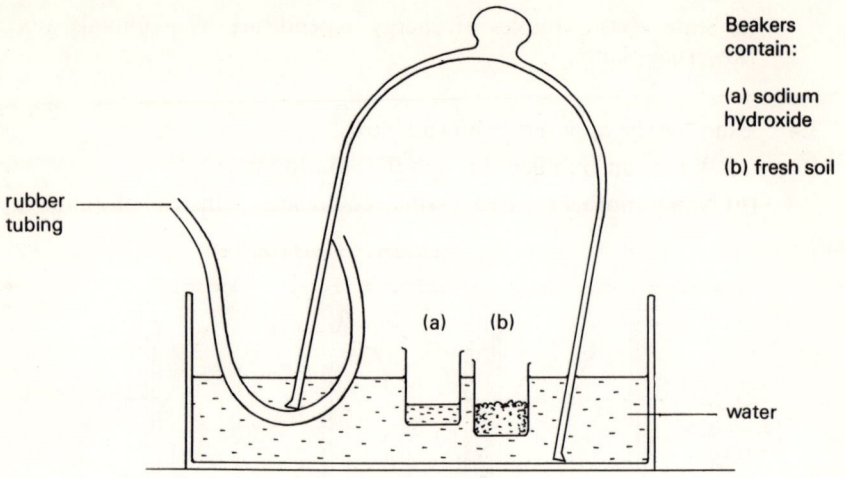

Beakers contain:

(a) sodium hydroxide

(b) fresh soil

(b) Briefly explain why a change is expected.

(c) What conclusion can be drawn from the experiment?
Soil may contain both aerobic and anaerobic organisms.

(d) If only aerobic organisms were present would you expect a different result in the above experiment?

(e) If only obligate anaerobes were present would you expect a different result?

(f) If the apparatus is left for several days the container with sodium hydroxide invariably sinks deeper into the water. Why is this?

23.8 Examine the illustration of an experiment shown below.

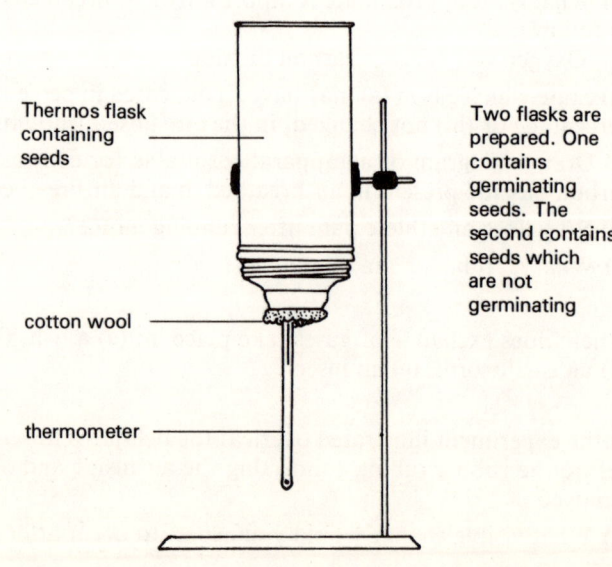

Two flasks are prepared. One contains germinating seeds. The second contains seeds which are not germinating

(a) What is the object of the experiment?
(b) Why are two flasks necessary?
(c) What treatment is given to the seeds before assembling the two flasks?
(d) Why are the flasks inverted?

23.9 Examine the apparatus illustrated below

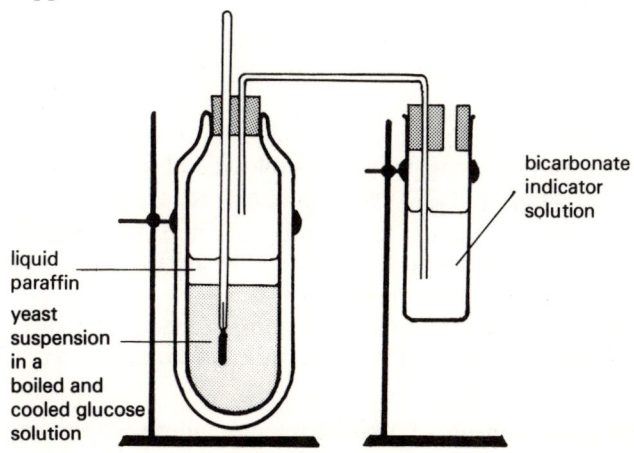

Time	Temperature °C
0	20.5
½ hour	21.4
1 hour	22.2
1½ hours	23.1
2 hours	24.0

(a) Why is it necessary to use glucose solution that has been (i) boiled, and (ii) cooled to suspend active yeast cells?
(b) What is the effect on the yeast suspension of a layer of liquid paraffin?
[(c)] (i) Plot a graph of the temperature change with time.
  (ii) State very approximately what you would expect the temperature in the flask to be after three hours of the experiment.
  (iii) Suggest TWO reasons why the temperature would not be expected to continue to increase in the way it did during the first two hours if the experiment were to be continued for two days.
[(d)] (i) The colour of the bicarbonate indicator solution changed from red to yellow during the period of the experiment. Why did this change occur?
  (ii) If clear calcium hydroxide solution had been used instead what changes would have been observed in this liquid?
[(e)] What control would be most suitable for this experiment?
[(f)] Write an equation in words or formulae that summarizes the biochemical change occurring in the flask that results in heat and a gas as waste products.

24 Homeostasis

24.1 Which of the following statements are CORRECT?

A Cells in the animal's body are surrounded by liquid called tissue fluid, and this tissue fluid supplies cells with food and oxygen and removes waste products.

B The tissue fluid is the internal environment of the body, and homeostasis is the name given to the process of maintenance of a constant internal environment.

C Homeostasis involves constant adjustment to the contents and the temperature of the body fluids (blood and tissue fluids).

D Homeostasis is achieved by a feed-back mechanism in which sense organs send information to the brain, the necessary corrective activity is dictated there, and commands relayed by nerves and/or hormones bring about changes by responding organs.

E Homeostasis is an entirely conscious activity that is carried out when the body is active but is discontinued at times of sleep and rest.

[24.2] The components of a feed-back mechanism are shown below:

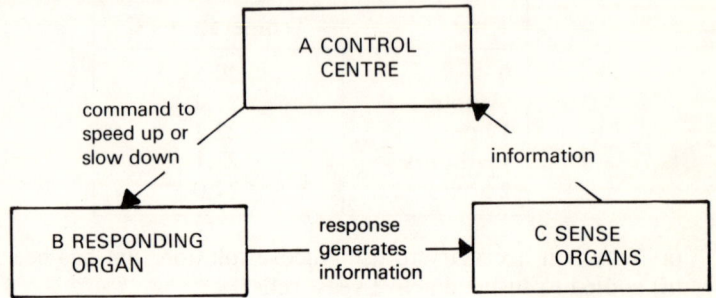

(a) When the mammal's body regulates its temperature from over-heating to normal body temperature which organs of the body act as A, B and C?

(b) When the mammal regulates its blood sugar level from below normal to normal level which organs of the body act as A, B and C?

25 The skin and body temperature control

25.1 Give structural differences between the following pairs: **(a)** dermis and epidermis, **(b)** sweat glands and sebaceous glands, **(c)** hair papilla and hair follicle, **(d)** capillary network and sub-cutaneous fat.

Excretion; kidney structure and function   47

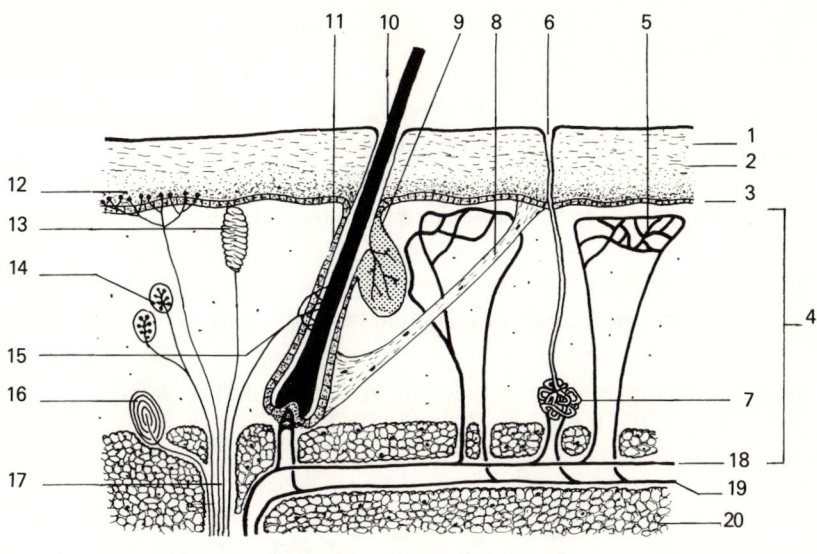

Skin in section

25.2   (a) Make a list of the labels appropriate to the structures numbered 1–20 in the diagram representing skin structure, as indicated.

(b) Give ONE beneficial property derived in each case from any three parts labelled.

(c) Name TWO components of the skin which are non-living.

(d) Name ONE component in which mitosis occurs.

25.3   (a) What part is played by the skin in cooling the body when it is overheated?

(b) Give the methods by which TWO other parts of the body also help to maintain body temperature.

25.4   (a) How would you determine the region of the body surface which is most sensitive to pricking?

(b) Why is the constant loss of skin cells not painful?

25.5   Give ONE beneficial effect and ONE harmful effect of sunlight on the skin.

26 Excretion; kidney structure and function

26.1   (a) What is the difference between 'egestion' and 'excretion'?

(b) When is oxygen excreted?

48 Excretion; kidney structure and function

26.2 (a) Indicate briefly how water leaves the following:
  (i) *Amoeba*,
  (ii) Green terrestrial plants,
  (iii) *Euglena* (or *Chlamydomonas*),
  (iv) A fish (or frog under water).
(b) Why is water lost during breathing by a bird?

26.3 Describe the route and give the processes involved for excretion of carbon dioxide from tissue of a mammal to the atmosphere.

26.4 (a) Using the apparatus drawn, how could air be breathed in through one flask only and out through the other flask?

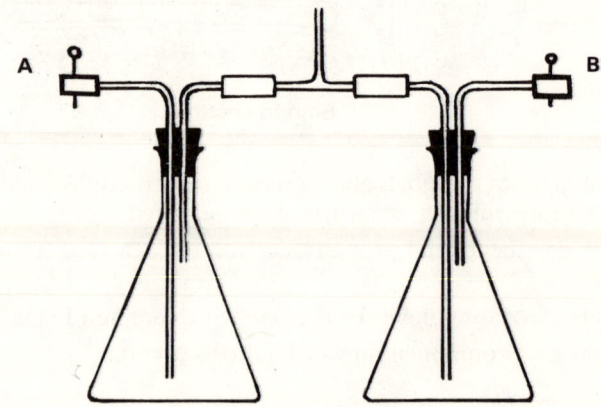

Excretion via lungs

(b) What colour change occurs if dry cobalt chloride paper is exposed to moist air?

[(c)] Where in the mammal's body are molecules of water formed as a waste product?

26.5 The diagram below shows a longitudinal section through a pig's kidney.

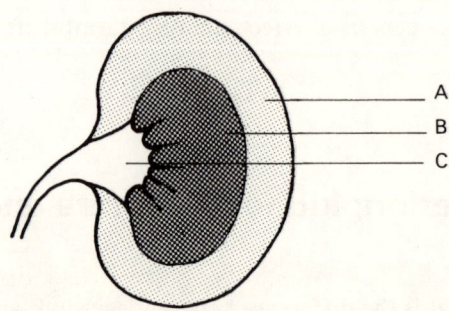

(a) List the names of the parts, A, B and C.

(b) In which part does water leave the blood, A, B or C?
(c) In which part does urea leave the blood, A, B or C?
(d) In which part does water re-enter the blood, A, B or C?
(e) In which part does urine leave the kidney, A, B or C?

26.6 The diagram below shows part of a kidney with a single kidney tubule in detail.

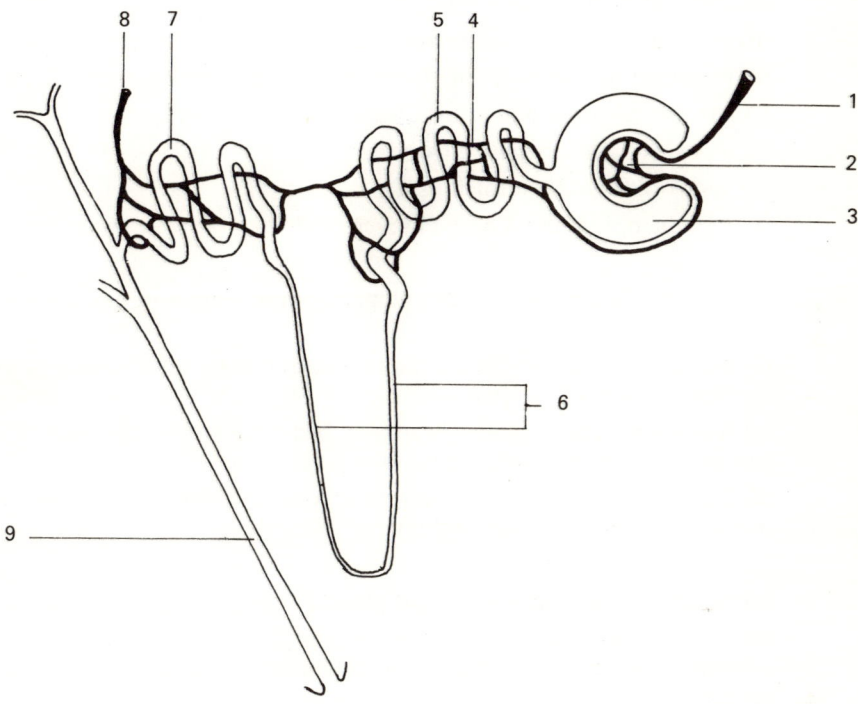

A single kidney tubule

(a) Make a list of the labels for the structures 1, 2, 3, 4, 5, 6, 7, 8 and 9.
(b) What process occurs in the parts of the kidney labelled 2–3, 4–5 and 7?

26.7 Give in correct sequence the names of the structures involved in the shortest route for a molecule of urea from the site of its manufacture until it reaches the bladder.

26.8 What is present in urine in addition to urea?

26.9 What is the basic principle of an artificial kidney?

26.10 Which test on urine could indicate that the person is diabetic?

27 Sensitivity

27.1 What is the difference between the following:
(a) sensitivity and response
(b) animal responses and plant responses
(c) a stimulus and an impulse
(d) a sense organ and an effector organ
(e) transport of hormones in plants and transport of hormones in animals
(f) a tropic response and a taxic response
(g) a positive and a negative tropism
(h) geotropism and phototropism
(i) thigmotropism and a nastic movement?

27.2 (a) How would you test whether all parts of the tongue are equally sensitive to salt?
(b) Make a drawing of the human tongue and map out the areas particularly sensitive to each of the four tastes.
(c) In winter a cold hammer-head may feel distinctly colder than its wooden handle at the same temperature. Why is this?
(d) Explain in general terms how you would test the sensitivity of different parts of the hand to touch stimulus.

27.3 (a) What are nastic movements of plants?
(b) Tulip flowers may close with certain conditions. Outline an experiment to test whether this response occurs with a change in temperature.

27.4 (a) Give TWO examples, ONE in plants and ONE in animals, of a response occurring in the organ stimulated.
(b) Give TWO examples, ONE in plants and ONE in animals, of a response occurring in an organ not initially stimulated.

27.5 (a) How does an etiolated shoot differ from a normal shoot? (See the diagram opposite.)
(b) What causes etiolation?
(c) If a shoot is illuminated by unilateral light which side elongates most?

27.6 (a) Show by means of a clinostat how you would use it to test the response of a shoot to light.
(b) For what points in the behaviour (response) of the shoot would you look?

27.7 (a) Show by means of a labelled drawing how a clinostat may be used to test whether a root responds to gravity.

(b) What precautions would you take to ensure good root growth?

(c) What other external factors might affect the response of roots?

27.8 (a) Devise a simple experiment to test whether pupil size of a human eye is affected by light intensity.

(b) What other stimulus can affect pupil size?

27.9 How would you attempt to determine the extent of the region of an oat coleoptile which is sensitive to light?

27.10 Bean seedlings with straight, short roots were selected and marked at 0.5 cm intervals.

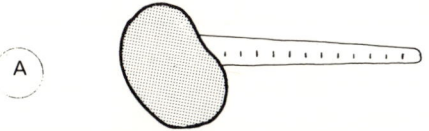

Ten of the beans were pinned to the surface of a slowly revolving clinostat, and ten were pinned to a similar stationary surface. After 36 hours the roots of one group of beans were as shown below:

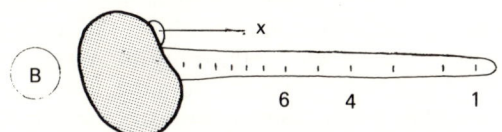

(a) What changes have occurred to the cells in:

(i) region 6   (ii) region 4   (iii) region 1?

(b) What is the structure X that is now appearing between the cotyledons?

(c) Would the root in B have been held stationary or revolving?

(d) Draw the condition of the other group of roots by means of one representative seedling, showing the resulting position of the markings too.

27.11 An experiment with the tips of cereal shoots is summarized in the diagrams below. Each shoot (or coleoptile) represents a batch of similarly treated plants.

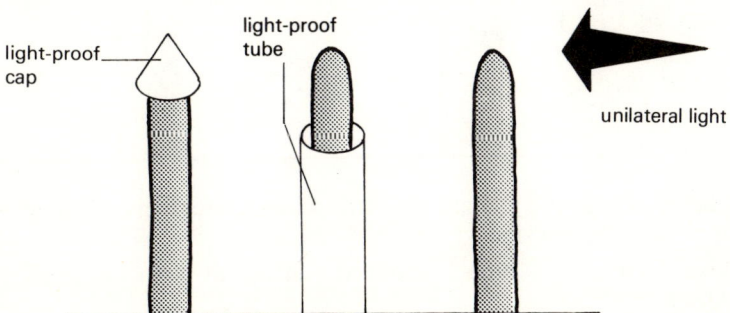

52 Sensitivity

(a) What results would you expect a few hours later? Give your answers by means of labelled drawings.

(b) What have you assumed about the area of sensitivity to light in the shoot?

27.12 Pieces of thin mica can be used to block the flow of chemicals from the tip of a shoot, and the following experiment was set up using mica.

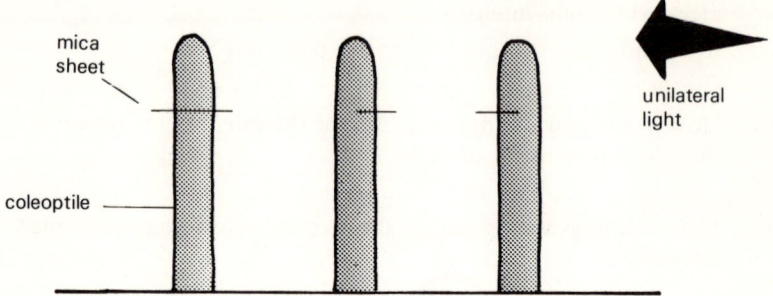

(a) What results would you anticipate four hours later? Give your answer by means of labelled drawings.

(b) What have you assumed about the movement of chemicals (growth hormones) from a unilaterally illuminated tip?

27.13 Plant growth hormones can diffuse into agar blocks from the cut tips of stems (or coleoptiles). An experiment with unilaterally illuminated cut tips of shoots is illustrated below. The growth hormone from the dark and the light sides is collected in separate agar blocks, using a mica sheet to separate.

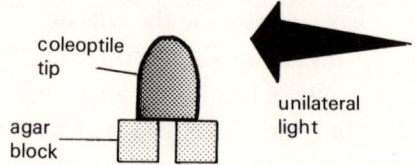

Subsequently the two blocks are placed asymetrically on the decapitated stumps of two separate stem tips, as shown.

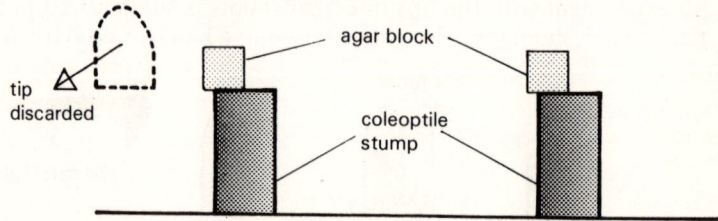

(a) What results would you anticipate four hours later? Give your answers by means of labelled drawings.

(b) What have you assumed about the effect of light on plant growth hormone?

28 The nervous system and sense organs; the reflex arc

28.1 The nerves of an animal are made of special cells.
(a) What are these cells called?
(b) What do they do?

28.2 Below are two different types of nerve cell.

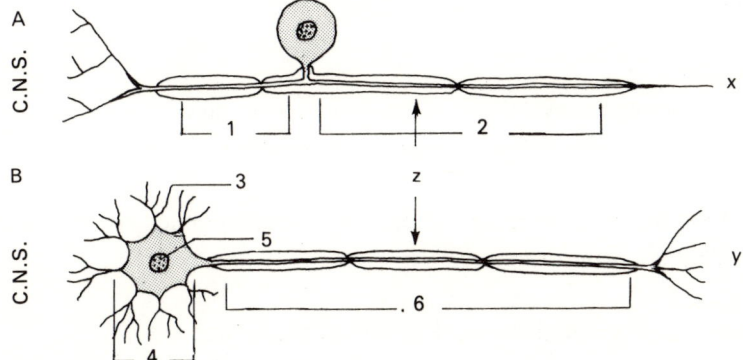

(a) Make a list of the labels of the structures indicated 1–6.
(b) State whether the direction of nervous connection in cell B is normally towards the cell body from Y, or in the opposite direction.
(c) Name a specific organ that might be connected at X and a different organ that might be connected at Y in the mammal's body.
(d) (i) What function does the structure Z perform?
   (ii) What is it made of?
(e) Where would you find a synapse?

28.3 Copy the diagram of the spinal cord in transverse section and complete and fully label the whole drawing to illustrate all structures concerned in the knee-jerk reflex action.

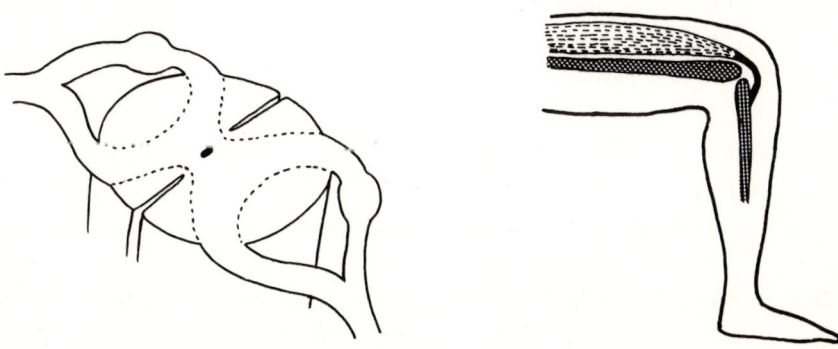

28.4 What is the difference between:
  (a) white matter and grey matter
  (b) the spinal cord and the spinal column
  (c) the central nervous system and the peripheral nerves?

28.5 (a) What is the difference between a reflex action and a conditioned reflex?
  (b) Which of the following are conditioned reflexes:
     (i) riding a bicycle
     (ii) producing saliva when chewing food
     (iii) enlargement of the pupil in weaker light
     (iv) coughing
     (v) writing
     (vi) blinking the eyelids when an object passes quickly near the eyes?
  (c) What general advantages result from reflexes?

[28.6] (a) What main function is performed by the autonomic nervous system?
  (b) What are proprioceptors?

28.7 Below is a diagramatic vertical section of the human brain

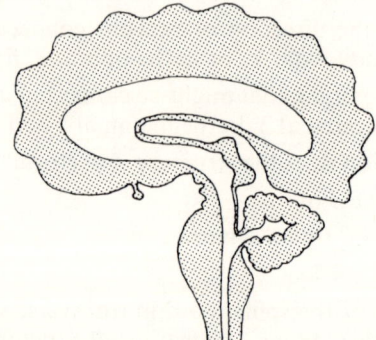

  (a) Copy the diagram and label
     (i) cerebral hemisphere
     (ii) cerebellum
     (iii) medulla.
  (b) What major functions are each of these three regions concerned with?
  (c) (i) Label on the drawing the pituitary body.
     (ii) What function does this gland perform?

28.8 Make a list of the labels appropriate to the structures numbered 1–14 in the diagram of a section through the human eye, at the top of the opposite page.

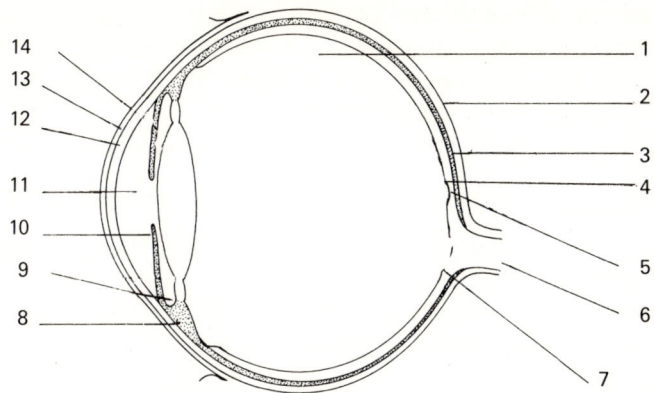

28.9 The drawing below shows the front view of the iris of a mammalian eye in low light.

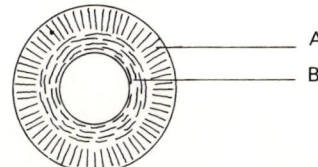

(a) State the names of the two types of muscle labelled A and B.
(b) Draw a similar view of the iris when it is exposed to bright light.
(c) Which muscle will have increased its contraction to achieve this change?
(d) What is meant by antagonistic muscles?

28.10 Below are drawings of sections through two eyes, each illustrating a different defect.

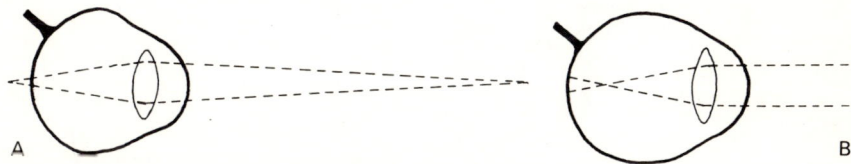

(a) In each case, what is the name of the defect shown?
(b) From the selection of different lenses below which lens would you use to correct defect A and defect B?

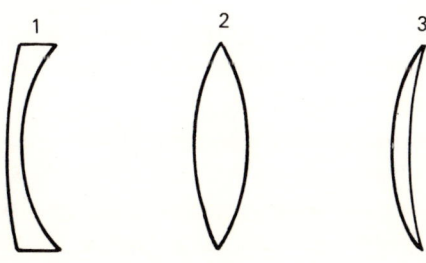

The nervous system and sense organs; the reflex arc

28.11 **(a)** How could you tell whether an unlabelled drawing of a section through the centre of an eye is a vertical or a horizontal section?

(b) Give ONE function in each case for the following parts of the eye: (i) aqueous humour, (ii) choroid, (iii) eyelid.

(c) What changes occur in the eyes, if a person reading a book suddenly falls asleep?

28.12 **(a)** Give TWO reasons why objects are seen more clearly via the central region of the retina.

(b) What do you consider to be the main difference (in structure or function) between the eye of man and that of (i) a caterpillar, (ii) a butterfly?

28.13 **(a)** Make a list of the names of the structures indicated in the diagram of the ear.

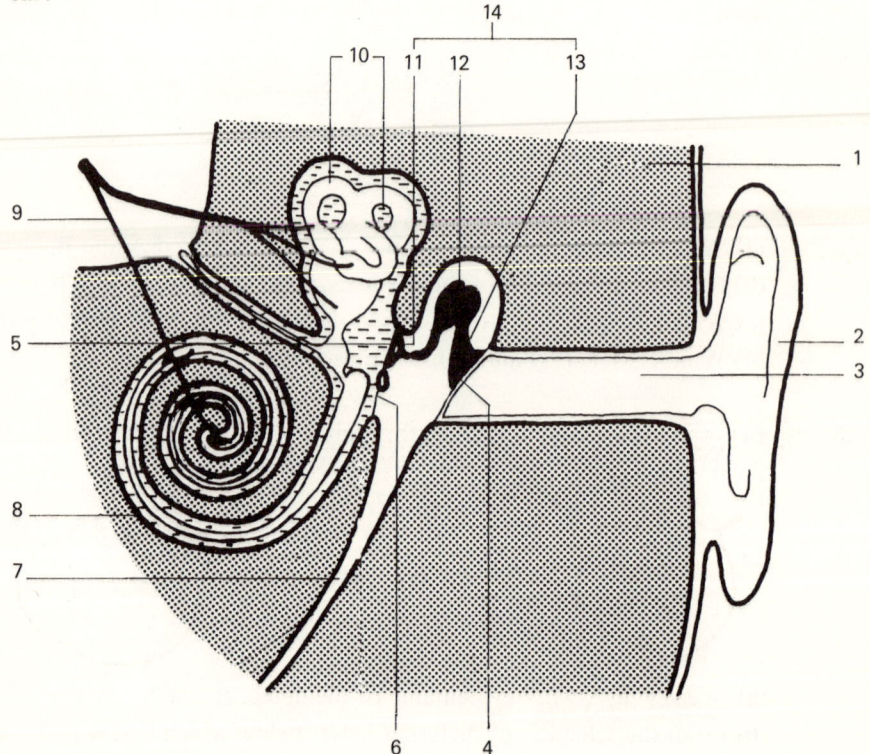

(b) Give ONE function for each of the following parts: (i) pinna, (ii) incus (anvil), (iii) horizontal semi-circular canal, (iv) utriculus, (v) eustachian tube.

28.14 **(a)** Describe an experiment to test whether the flavour of food is only partially detected by the tongue.

(b) What differences in addition to shape can be detected in various objects solely by handling them?

29 Co-ordination by nerves and hormones; behaviour

29.1 Give one example of a response by an endocrine organ (hormone-producing gland) following a stimulus perceived through the nervous system.

29.2 What is the difference between the following:
(a) a hormone and an enzyme
(b) the action of thyroxine and the action of adrenaline
(c) migration and hibernation
(d) instinct (innate behaviour) and intelligence?

29.3 (a) What do you understand by a 'feed-back' mechanism?
(b) Outline briefly a feed-back mechanism which helps to maintain human body temperature.
(c) Give one difference in the means of body temperature control by birds and by man.

29.4 Indicate briefly the development in the whole body or parts of the body which is brought about by secretions by each of the following: (a) pituitary gland, (b) pancreas, (c) gonads.

29.5 (a) Why can we ride bicycles without conscious thought of balancing?
(b) What connection may exist between leg movement in walking and the knee-jerk reflex?

29.6 How would you expect the amount of sugar in your blood to be affected by the following:
(a) digestion of carbohydrate
(b) formation of glycogen
(c) running
(d) secretion of insulin
(e) secretion of adrenalin
(f) kidney action?

29.7 (a) What effect may the removal of a developing terminal bud of a woody twig have on other buds of the same twig? Give an explanation.
(b) Many seeds do not germinate as soon as they are formed and dispersed. Why not?

29.8 (a) How would you carry out a simple test of the effect of thyroxin on tadpole metamorphosis?

(b) Why would you need a 'control'?

(c) What control would you plan for this experiment?

[29.9] The effect of unilateral light on plants growing in the absence of gravity can be investigated with the apparatus shown below:

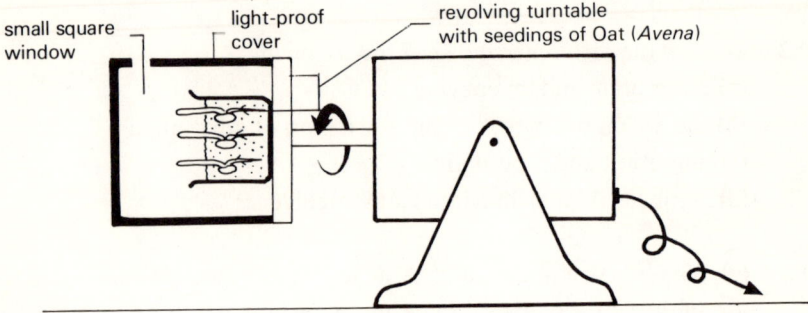

(a) What results would you expect in the growth of the shoots (coleoptiles)?

(b) How would you use this apparatus to investigate shoot growth when the stimuli of gravity and unilateral light are opposed?

30 Movement; muscles and joints

30.1 (a) What advantages may be gained by organisms from their ability to move? Give examples.

(b) State the common difference in the movement of plants and of animals.

30.2 What is the difference between:
(a) bone and cartilage
(b) endoskeleton and exoskeleton
(c) tendon and ligament
(d) clavicle and sternum
(e) pectoral and pelvic girdle
(f) sliding joints and ball and socket joints?

30.3 State briefly one difference in the movement of the following pairs of organisms:
(a) walking by an insect and a dog
(b) swimming by a fish and a human
(c) crawling by an earthworm and a housefly maggot

(d) flight by a bat and a bee

(e) movement by *Euglena* (or *Chlamydomonas*) and *Amoeba*.

30.4 (a) By means of a carefully labelled drawing, show how the arm muscles flex your arm at the elbow.

(b) What type of joint occurs at the elbow?

30.5 (a) What do you understand by Brownian movement?

(b) How would you demonstrate Brownian movement?

[30.6] Locomotion is shown by microscopic plants and animals as well as by almost all larger animals.

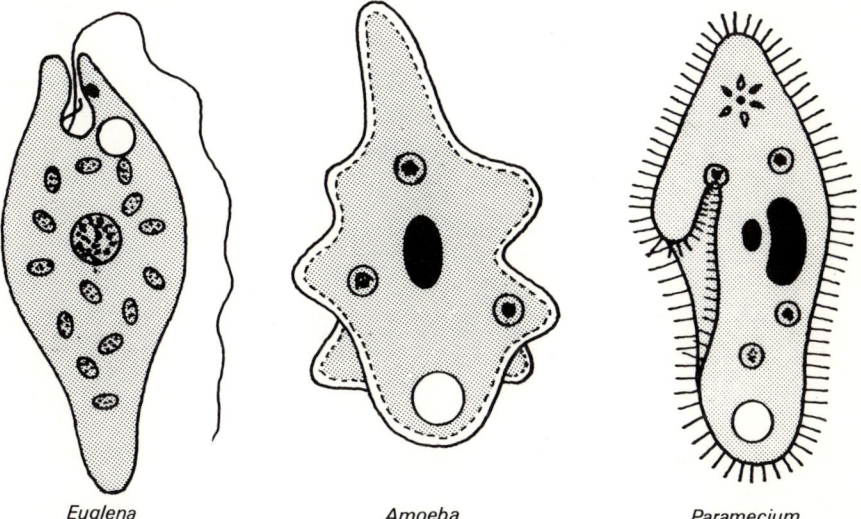

Euglena Amoeba Paramecium

(a) Copy the diagram of *Euglena* and annotate it to describe how this organism swims forwards.

(b) Indicate with an arrow on your drawing the direction of movement of *Euglena* as shown.

(c) Copy the grid and complete it to contrast the methods of locomotion and of feeding in *Amoeba* and *Paramecium*.

	Amoeba	*Paramecium*
locomotion		
feeding		

(d) One type of cell in the mammal also illustrates amoeboid movement. Which type of cell is it?

31 Growth

31.1 (a) What do you understand by the term 'growth'?

(b) Is it possible to get an increase in size but a decrease of (i) fresh weight, (ii) dry weight? (Explain your answer.)

(c) Which two aspects of growth are depicted in the diagram below?

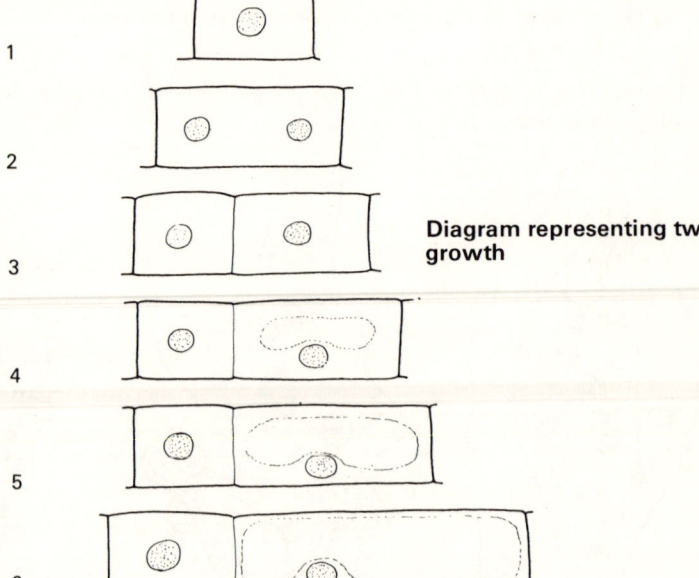

Diagram representing two aspects of growth

31.2 How does growth of most animals differ from that of most plants?

31.3 What disadvantage to an *Amoeba* cell would develop if it grew continuously and failed to divide?

31.4 (a) How would you investigate the changes in dry weight of groundsel plants for one complete life-cycle?

(b) Draw a graph as outlined below to indicate dry weight changes during the life of an annual plant. Annotate the graph to indicate stages in the life-cycle of the plant.

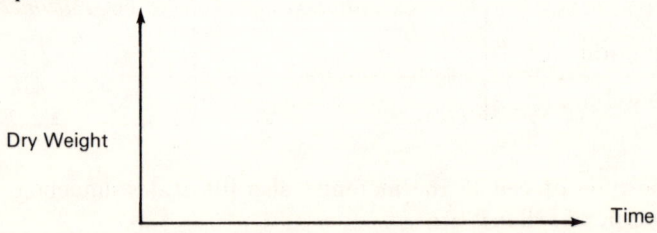

(c) Draw a graph of the measured height of a typical human male over the period 0–21 years. Annotate features of the curve that highlight differences between human growth and tree height over the same period.

31.5 How would you modify the apparatus drawn to obtain a continuous record of rate of growth over 24 hours?

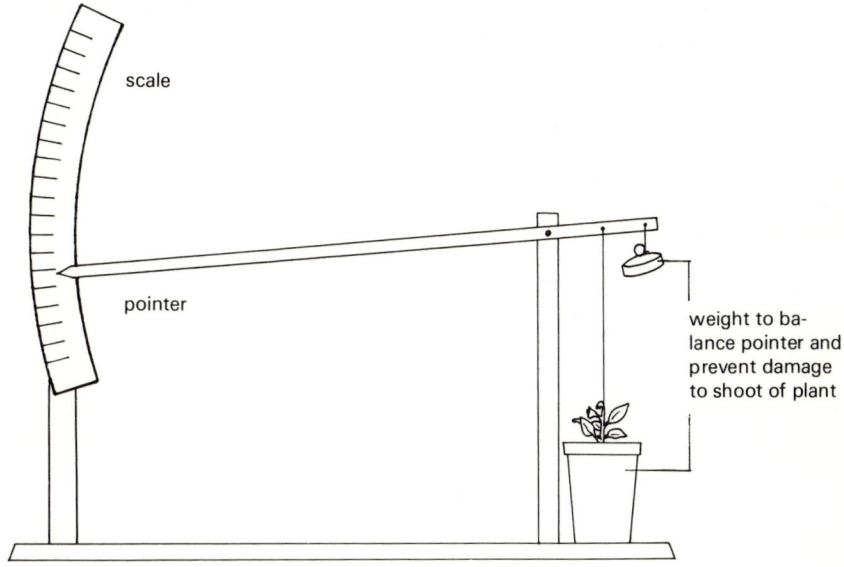

A simple growth lever

31.6 State briefly how (why) each of the following would increase or decrease the rate of growth of green plants, assuming other factors to be 'ideal' for growth:
(a) a rise of temperature from 10°C to 20°C
(b) a shortage of calcium
(c) an excess of nitrogen
(d) an absence of carbon dioxide in the air
(e) a shortage of water
(f) an absence of light for 24 hours.

31.7 (a) Indicate briefly how you would investigate the exact region of growth of a young hyacinth (or similar) leaf.
(b) You are required to investigate the region of stem growth (elongation) in a batch of young seedlings.
   (i) What technique would you use?
   (ii) What precautions would you take?

31.8 (a) How does a woody shoot increase in girth?
(b) Which plants stop growing at maturity?

32 Secondary thickening in plants; perennation and hibernation

32.1 (a) Which types of plant undergo secondary thickening?

(b) Show by labelled diagrams how the internal structure of a woody twig differs from that of a herbaceous dicotyledonous stem as seen with a lens.

(c) What is an annual ring? State where and how it is formed.

32.2 (a) State TWO useful functions served in each case by (i) secondary xylem of a stem, and (ii) cork.

(b) How does air get to the active cells in a woody twig?

32.3 (a) What is the difference between heartwood and sapwood?

(b) Where is food stored in a tree?

(c) Where is a primary ray situated in (i) a woody stem, (ii) a woody root?

32.4 Give ONE different example for each of the following: (a) deciduous tree, (b) evergreen tree, (c) stem tuber, (d) root tuber, (e) corm, (f) bulb, (g) rhizome, (h) tap root.

32.5 Make a list of the SIX distinct features indicated in the drawing of a winter twig.

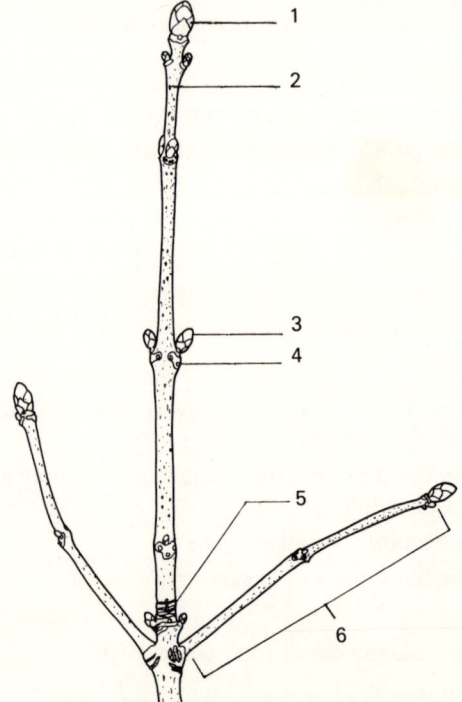

32.6 (a) Define (i) perennation, and (ii) hibernation.

(b) Give TWO similarities in the two processes 'perennation' and 'hibernation'.

32.7 (a) How does hibernation differ from sleep?

(b) Which of the following groups of animals contain several hibernating species?

insects, mammals, reptiles, fish, snails, amphibia, birds.

32.8 (a) List the names of the structures indicated on the diagram of a bulb and a corm.

(b) Draw ONE of them to show the structure after flowering time.

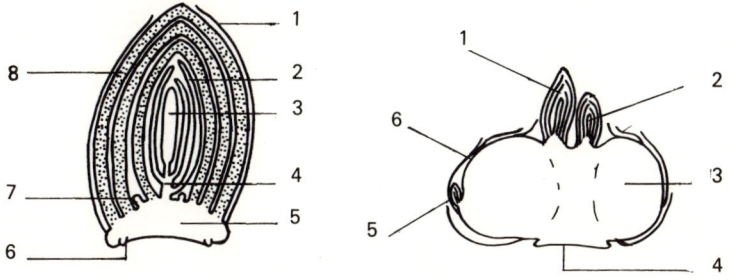

32.9 (a) What are the main differences between woody and herbaceous perennials?

(b) In what form do annual plants survive the winter?

33 Reproduction: cell division, replicative and reductive

33.1 (a) What is the main difference between sexual and asexual reproduction?

(b) What are the special advantages gained by an organism from the following:

    (i) asexual reproduction

    (ii) sexual reproduction?

33.2 (a) What do you understand by the terms

    (i) binary fission,

    (ii) budding?

(b) Make labelled drawings of two different animals

    (i) one carrying out binary fission, and

    (ii) one carrying out budding.

33.3 Below is a drawing of a well-known flowering plant that vegetatively reproduces with or without the intervention of man.

(a) Make a list of the structures indicated in the drawing.

(b) Describe concisely how, with time, more than one independent plant is formed.

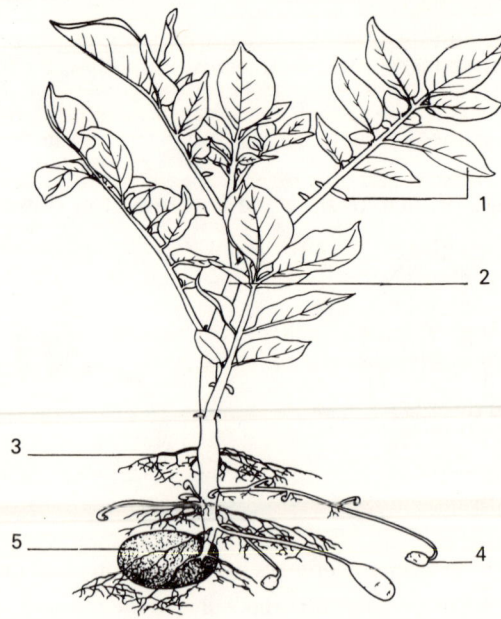

33.4 Complex animals such as fish, birds and mammals do not reproduce asexually, but some insects do produce offspring from one parent.

(a) What is this process called?

(b) Name an insect that reproduces by this method, and state where you can find and observe this organism near your school or home.

(c) At what stage in the life-cycle does this form of reproduction occur, and what advantage does this form of reproduction confer?

(d) Name a common predator of the insect you describe.

33.5 (a) Is reproduction by spores referred to as vegetative propagation or as asexual reproduction?

(b) Name a non-flowering green plant that reproduces by airborne spores, and state what habitat you would find this in.

33.6 Give an example of:
(a) an animal having external fertilization,

(b) an animal having internal fertilization but mainly external embryonic development,

(c) an animal having internal fertilization and internal embryonic development.

Reproduction; cell division, replicative and reductive 65

33.7 State clearly the differences between the following pairs of terms:
(a) gamete and gonad
(b) zygote and embryo
(c) gestation and fertilization
(d) foetus and placenta
(e) complete and incomplete metamorphosis in insects.

[33.8] (a) The cell nucleus contains instructions or information in chemical form. This is contained in what structures?

(b) These structures can only be seen at a particular time in the life cycle. When are they visible?

(c) Two different types of cell division are observed in cells: *replicative division* in which the number of information structures in the daughter cells is exactly the same as in the parent cells, and *reductive division* in which four cells are formed from each 'parent' cell and the number of information structures per cell is exactly half that in the parent cells.
  (i) Which of these two divisions is associated with egg and sperm production in mammals?
  (ii) Which division occurs during growth of body tissues?

(d) Below are shown six stages of the replicative division, lettered A — F, but in the wrong order. Put the letters in correct sequence to represent the division as it occurs in cells.

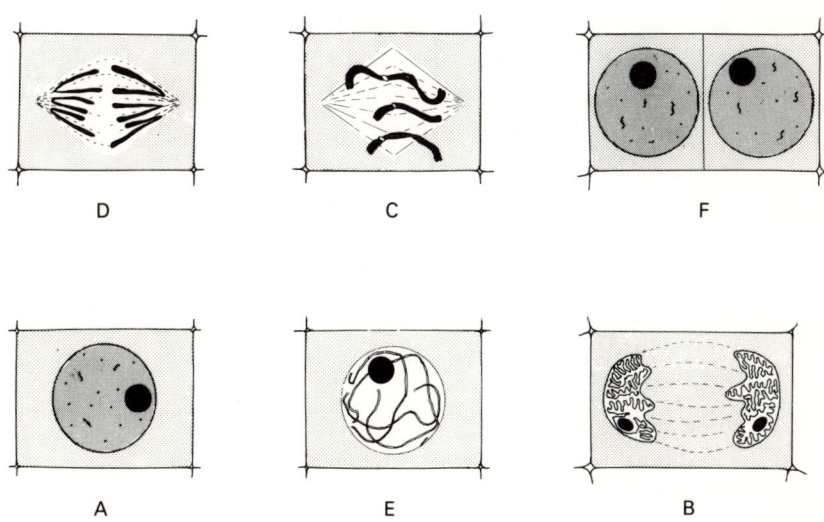

Question 33.9 overleaf.

33.9 State concisely how the male gamete travels to the female gamete in (a) *Spirogyra*, (b) a flowering plant, (c) *Hydra*, (d) a named fish.

34 Flower structure, pollination, fertilization, fruit formation

34.1 (a) Make a list of the structures indicated in the 'half-flower' drawing of the buttercup.

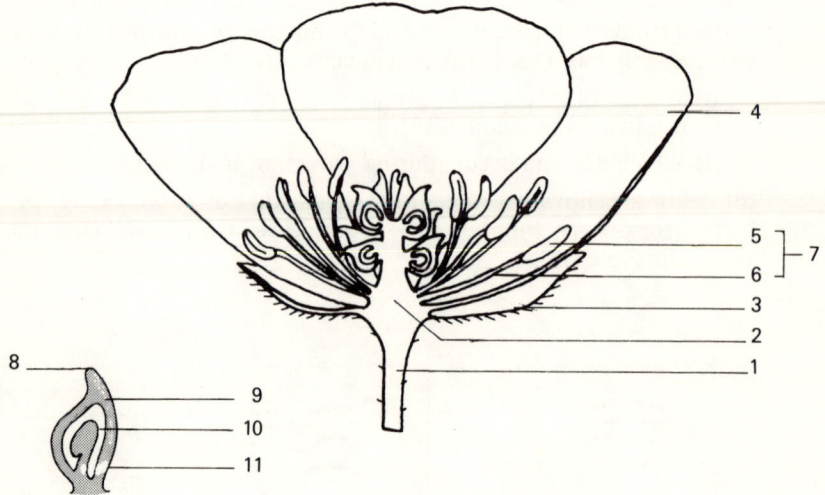

(b) What insects can visit this flower?
(c) What features of the flower attract the insects?
(d) How is pollination achieved in this flower?
(e) State two major dangers to which the flower is particularly vulnerable.

34.2 Show by means of concise definitions or by labelled drawings that you understand the differences between the following pairs of terms:
(a) solitary flower and inflorescence
(b) flower and floret
(c) regular and irregular (zygomorphic) flowers
(d) sepal and petal
(e) petal and corolla
(f) pistil and stamen

(g) carpel and gynoecium
(h) pollination and fertilization
(i) fruit and seed.

34.3 (a) For what purpose does a bee visit a flower?

(b) If a poppy flower produces 100 seeds, what do you know about the amount of pollen involved in pollination?

34.4 (a) What is the difference between cross-pollination and self-pollination?

(b) Is pollen shed towards the centre or towards the outside, in (i) the buttercup, (ii) the daisy?

(c) Give one reason in each case why cross-pollination is likely to occur in (i) the buttercup, (ii) the daisy.

34.5 Below is a drawing of a half-flower of white deadnettle:

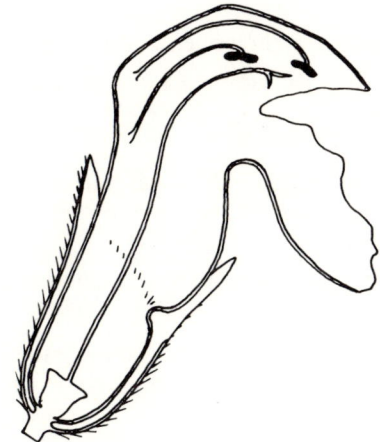

(a) Where would you expect to find nectar in this flower?

(b) What sort of insects benefit from a visit to this flower?

(c) Which structures help to exclude other insect visitors?

(d) Stamens in the flower shed their pollen well before the stigma surface is exposed for pollination. How then is pollination achieved?

(e) State two structural features you would describe as advanced, and that are not a feature of the buttercup flower.

[34.6] Pea plants have been used in many breeding (genetics) experiments.

(a) What steps and precautions are necessary in order to cross-pollinate two selected sweet-pea plants?

(b) In later experiments the progeny (offspring) are often allowed to self-fertilize. What precautions are necessary to see that this occurs in a sweet-pea?

34.7 Below is a drawing of a single grass flower (one of the bracts has been removed to expose the centre of the flower).

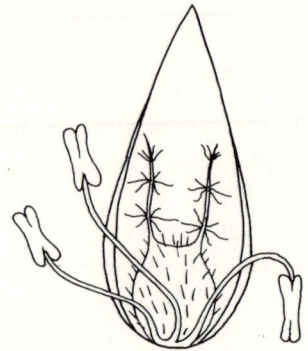

By careful examination of the above drawing, and using your biological knowledge list FOUR features of the grass flower that contrast with those of the white deadnettle flower and which you see as adaptations to wind pollination.

34.8 (a) What developments of the pollen grain follow successful pollination?

(b) What is the difference between a pollen grain and a male gamete of a flowering plant?

34.9 (a) Indicate briefly what happens to the following parts of any *named* plant after successful pollination: (i) calyx, (ii) corolla, (iii) stamens, (iv) ovary wall, (v) ovule.

(b) Comment on the fact that apples sometimes are very lop-sided.

[34.10] Name TWO different plants which produce either seedless fruits or fruits without viable seed. How has this sterility come about?

34.11 Copy the diagram of part of a pea flower.

(a) Mark the position of a female cell (egg cell).

(b) Add to the drawing to show how a male gamete reaches the female cell from the stigma.

(c) After fertilization what TWO quite distinct structures develop in the ovule as it becomes a seed?

(d) Why are seeds of various types a major ingredient of the diet of so many different animals?

35 Seed dispersal; seed germination

35.1 Many plants have an efficient seed dispersal mechanism.

(a) What advantages may result from efficient seed dispersal?

(b) How may dispersal occur with indehiscent fruits? Give two distinct methods.

(c) (i) Why are some seeds which are eaten not harmed in the alimentary canal of the animals?

(ii) Name a seed or fruit which does not survive in a bird's alimentary canal.

35.2 For each of the following diagrams (i) list the names of the features indicated, and (ii) write concise notes to indicate the dispersal mechanism.

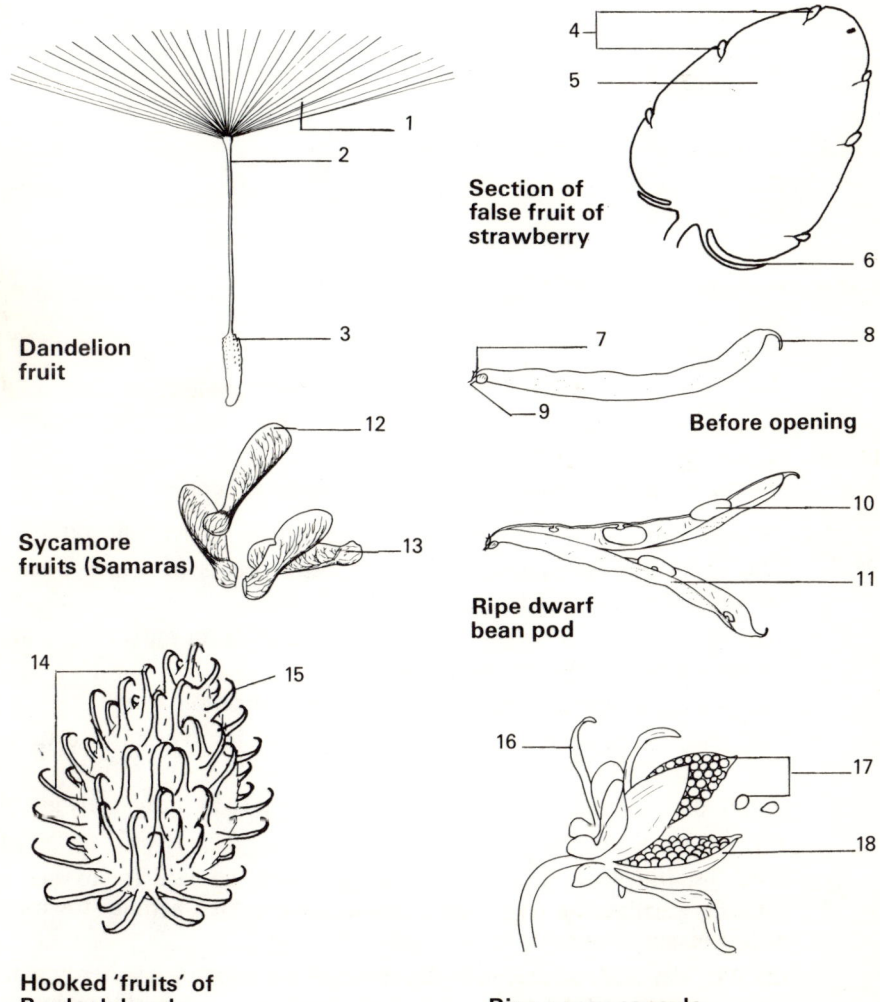

70 Seed dispersal; seed germination

35.3 (a) Make a list of the labels to the structures numbered 1–12 on the diagram of the cut maize fruit and the broad bean seeds.

(b) State TWO differences in structure between seeds (or fruits) of a cultivated grass (e.g. maize) and a member of the pea family (broad bean).

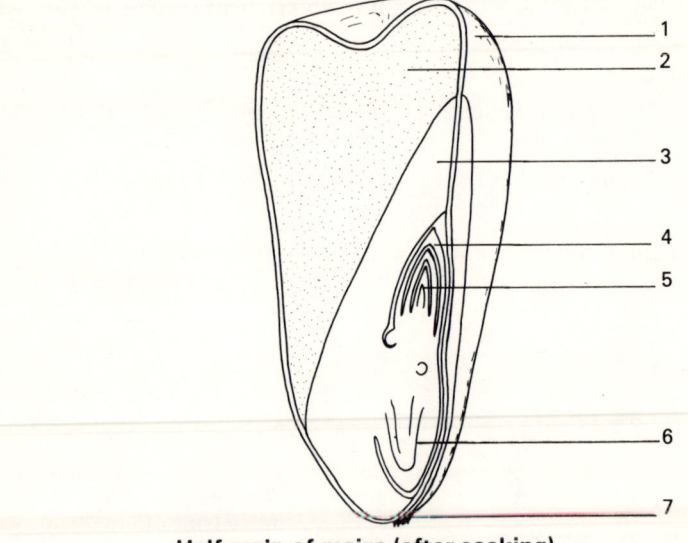

Half grain of maize (after soaking)

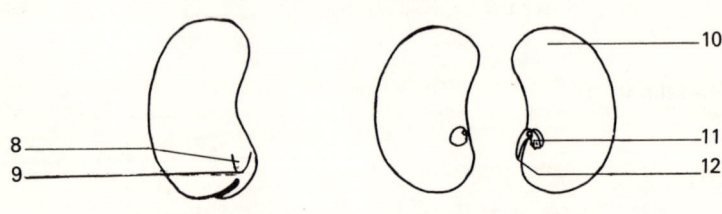

Soaked broad bean   Broad bean opened

35.4 Stored seeds are dry and may contain as little as 10 per cent water.

(a) What approximate percentage of water occurs in healthy, germinating seedlings?

(b) Name TWO other types of substances, apart from water, that germinating seeds take from their environment.

(c) Why does low temperature slow down seed germination?

(d) If the temperature becomes abnormally high it can be harmful to seedlings. Why is this?

(e) State FOUR important uses that water is put to in the actively growing cell.

35.5 The apparatus (A) opposite is concerned with the need for oxygen by seeds during germination. Alkaline pyrogallol has a high affinity for oxygen and absorbs and thus removes this gas from the air.

(a) An identical apparatus B was set up, but it contained water in place of the alkaline pyrogallol solution. What is the value of this additional apparatus?

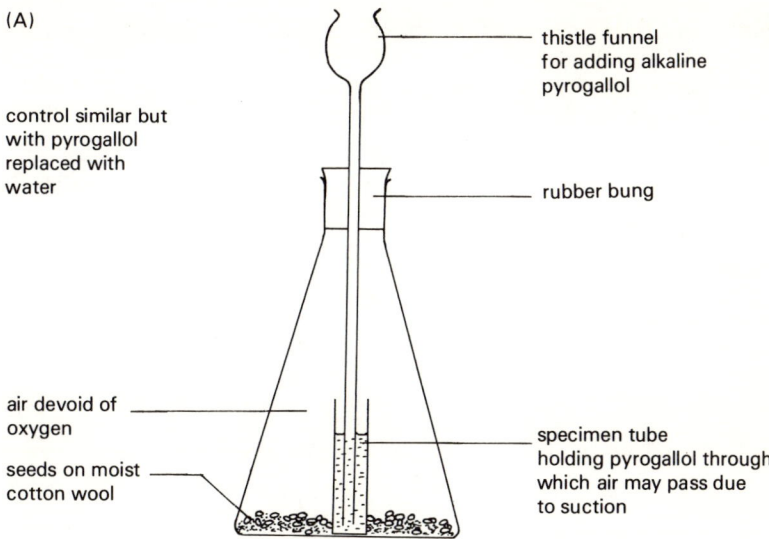

(b) What changes would occur to the air in the experiment (A) after it is set up?

(c) What changes do you expect in the moist seeds in (A) and (B) after some days?

(d) (i) How do some living things obtain energy in the absence of air?

(ii) Name an organism that you know can respire without oxygen.

35.6 A tomato is cut open and half of the seeds are removed and washed in running water for one hour. These give 90 per cent germination. The rest of the seeds, unwashed, give a 'nil' germination, under otherwise similar conditions. What deduction can you make?

[35.7] **(a)** How would you use the starch jelly to test for amylase (diastase) in germinating seeds?

(b) State TWO processes which must have occurred if it is found that starch is not uniformly distributed in the jelly at the end of the experiment.

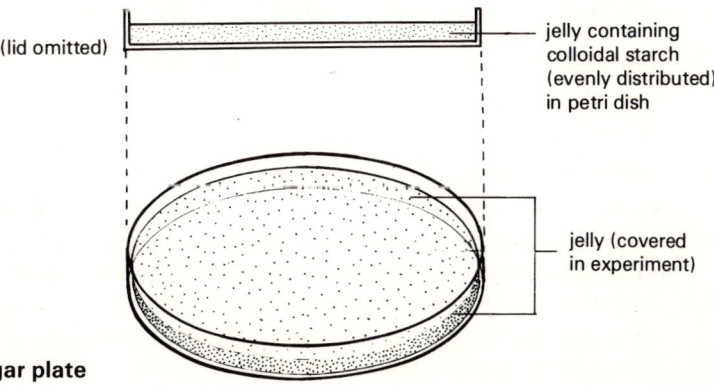

Starch-agar plate

72 Seed dispersal; seed germination

35.8 **(a)** List the names of the structures in the drawings of germinating broad bean and dwarf bean.

(b) What is the key difference between these two types of germination?

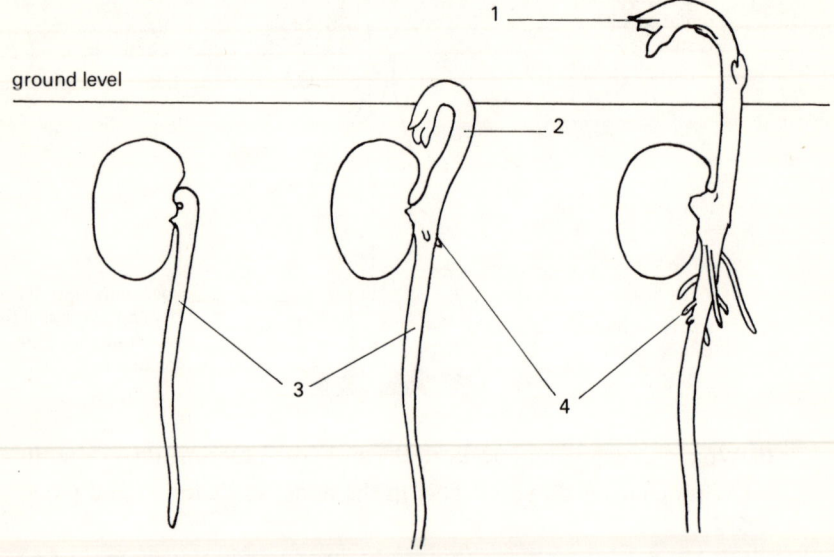

Germinating broad bean

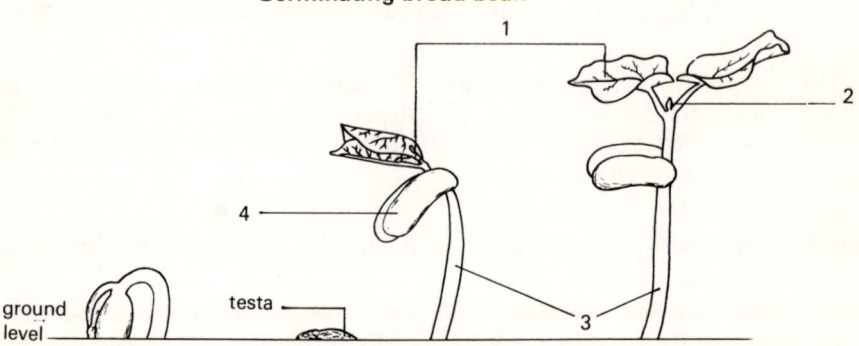

Germinating dwarf bean

35.9 Examine the drawings of early stages in germination of maize and sycamore opposite.

(a) What type of root system does the maize plant develop and how does this differ from that of the sycamore?

(b) What difference can be observed in the behaviour of the cotyledon(s) in maize and sycamore during germination?

(c) What type of vein arrangement occurs in the leaves of grasses, and how does this differ from that in broad-leaved plants such as sycamore?

(d) When the food store of the seed is used up how do these plants obtain (i) sugar, and (ii) protein?

Seed dispersal; seed germination 73

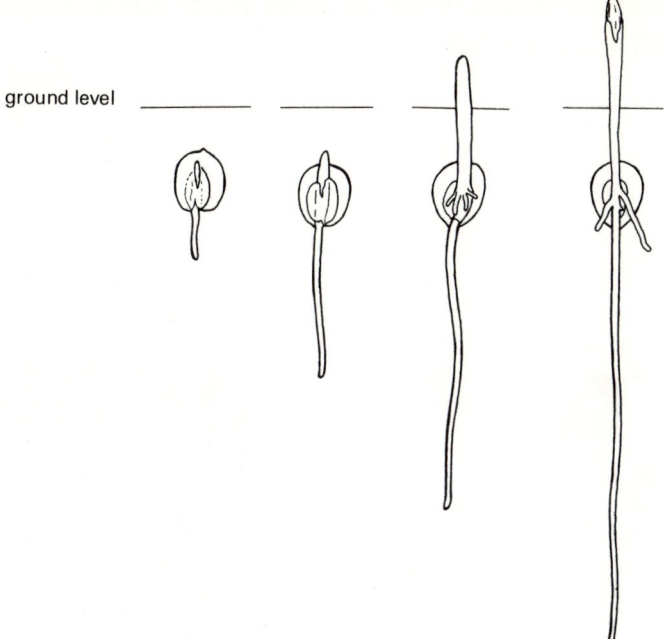

Germinating maize

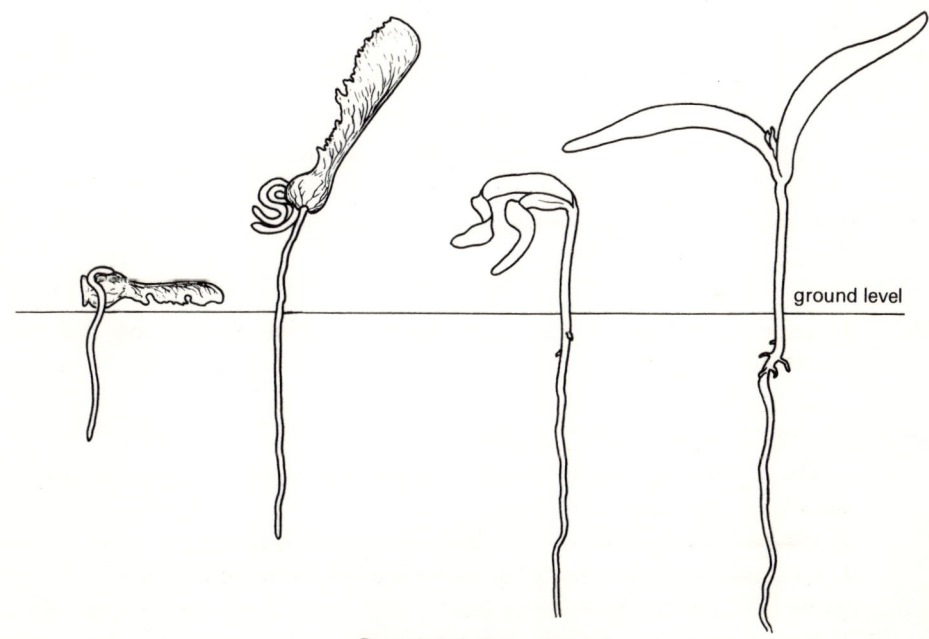

Germinating sycamore

36 Sexual reproduction in vertebrates; embryology; child birth; parental care

36.1 (a) List the structures indicated in the drawings of human male and female reproductive organs.

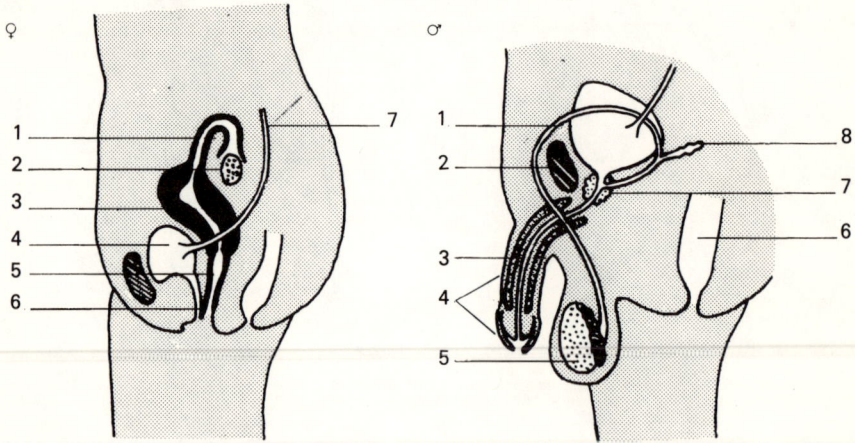

(b) Where in the human body are
  (i) sperms produced
  (ii) sperms stored
  (iii) eggs produced
  (iv) eggs or an egg fertilized
  (v) the first steps in the development of a fertilized egg
  (vi) the later stages in the development of the foetus?

36.2 By means of large labelled drawings show the differences between male and female gametes of a mammal.

36.3 State concisely how mating is achieved by (a) birds, (b) the frog, and (c) a mammal.

36.4 Comment on key points of biological interest in the following facts:

A The animals in one litter (or seeds in one fruit) can differ in their paternal origin.

B Internal fertilization occurs in birds but not in frogs.

C In humans a large embryo develops from a minute egg, but a bird's egg needs to be larger than a frog's egg.

D In many countries people are not permitted to marry their relatives.

36.5 The diagram shows the position of the human foetus shortly before birth.

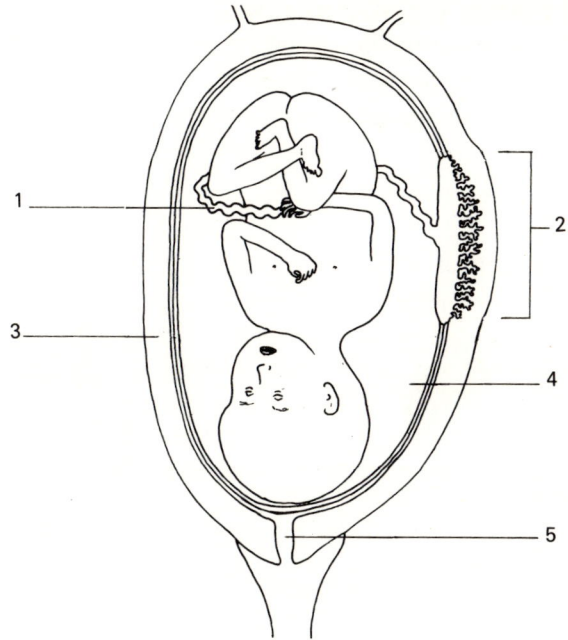

(a) Make a list of the labels for the structures 1–5.
(b) How does an expectant mother usually know that child-birth has started?
(c) Distinguish between the terms (i) embryo, (ii) foetus, and (iii) baby.
(d) What is the value to the developing foetus of the structures labelled 4, and 2.
(e) Copy the diagram below, showing part of the uterus wall during pregnancy. Annotate your drawing to describe the role of the placenta in the life of the embryo.

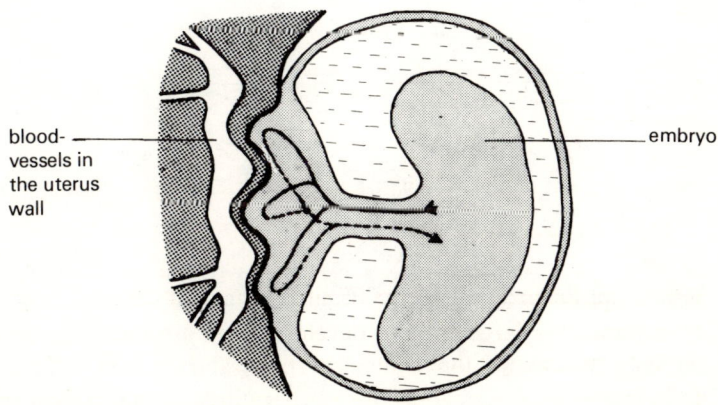

76 Simple green plants

36.6 Why should expectant mothers do the following things?
(a) stop smoking cigarettes
(b) ensure adequate intake of calcium
(c) reduce any alcohol consumption
(d) attend ante-natal clinics.

[36.7] What is genetic counselling?

36.8 Julius Caesar apparently made a method of entry into the world famous. What is this method, and why is it performed?

36.9 (a) What change occurs in the baby's source of oxygen at the time of birth?
(b) What happens to the membranes and the placenta after birth of an offspring?
(c) Outline TWO ways in which a mammal you have studied demonstrates parental care.

37 Simple green plants, *Spirogyra* and *Pleurococcus*

37.1 (a) Give THREE reasons why *Spirogyra* is classified as a plant.
(b) How would you be able to identify fresh *Spirogyra* at the pond-side, without the use of a microscope?
(c) List the labels to structures 1–8 shown in the diagram of a cell of *Spirogyra* filament.

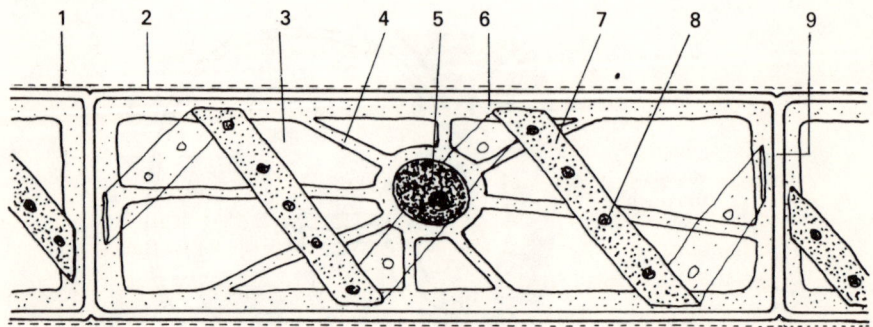

37.2 (a) *Spirogyra* is common in ponds in spring and summer. Where and how does it overwinter?

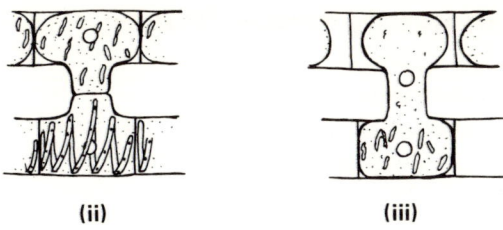

(ii)   (iii)

(b) Two stages in conjugation are drawn and labelled (ii) and (iii). Make your own drawings of stages (i) and (iv) to illustrate the onset and the completion of conjugation. Annotate your drawings.

37.3 **(a)** How does growth of a *Spirogyra* filament differ from the growth of a fungal hypha?

(b) (i) How would you establish that gas given off by *Spirogyra* in the light is rich in oxygen?

(ii) How would you then establish that light is essential for gas production?

37.4 Parts of the surface of tree trunks, wooden posts, or walls may appear green due to a surface layer of the alga called *Pleurococcus*.

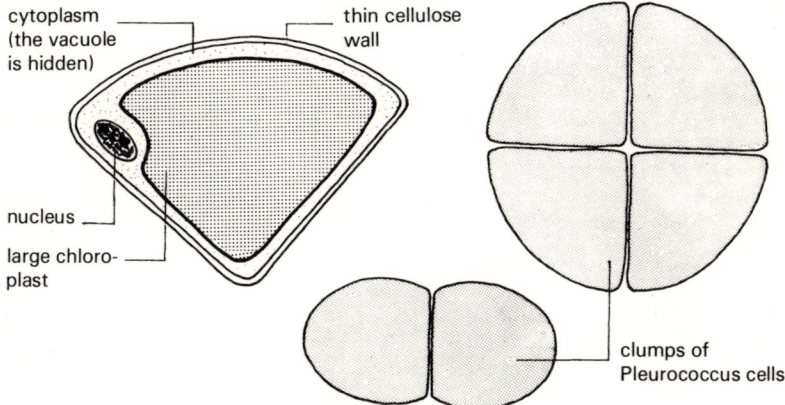

Cells of Pleurococcus viewed under the microscope

(a) What does this plant require from its environment in order to be able to survive and make its own food?

(b) What conditions may be harmful and kill *Pleurococcus*?

(c) Cells of *Pleurococcus* often appear clumped in groups of two or four cells, rather than as separate single cells. Why may this be the case?

(d) (i) How would you investigate an uneven distribution of green algae around a trunk at one metre from the ground?

(ii) How would you present your results?

(iii) If the distribution is uneven which environmental factors do you recommend be measured to help you account for the distribution?

38 Common mould fungi, *Mucor*

38.1 Mould fungi grow on damp organic matter. If a slice of wholemeal bread and a slice of modern white bread are dampened and exposed to the air which type of bread is colonised first by fungi, and why?

38.2 (a) In what way is *Mucor* 'plant-like' and in what way does it differ from plants like *Spirogyra*?

(b) What gas leaves *Mucor* hyphae

   (i) by day or in the light,

   (ii) by night or in the dark?

(c) Give one advantage and one disadvantage to man caused by growth of the fungus *Mucor*.

38.3 Copy the diagram of stages in the life history of *Mucor*. Complete them by labelling your drawings and add one further drawing to represent completion of asexual reproduction and a second to complete sexual reproduction.

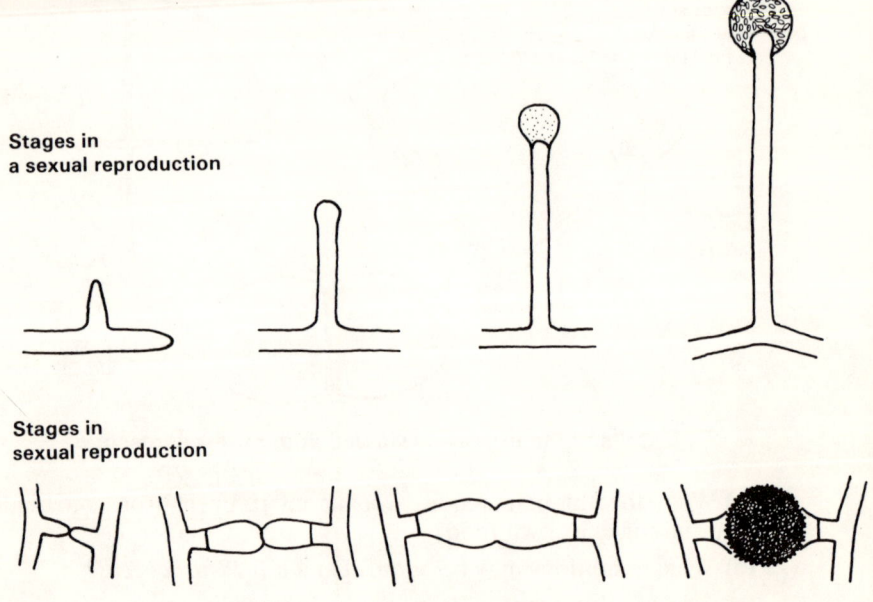

38.4 State ONE basic difference, in each case, between:

(a) a hypha and a mycelium,

(b) a gametangium and a fusion cell (zygote),

(c) a zygospore and a sporangium,

(d) a saprophyte and a parasite.

[38.5] **(a)** Where in your garden at home or at school would you be most likely to find *Mucor* growing?

(b) Once you had found *Mucor* growing how would you grow an isolated or 'pure' culture in your school laboratory?

39 Mosses and ferns; conifers

39.1 Mosses and ferns are non-flowering plants that reproduce by spores, but they often grow in different habitats

(a) In what sort of habitat are you more likely to find a moss?

(b) Where are ferns commonly found growing?

(c) Flowering plants obtain water and mineral salts from the soil via their root system. How are water and ions obtained by (i) a moss, and (ii) a fern?

(d) Mosses are more at risk from atmospheric pollution than are ferns. Why is this so?

39.2 **(a)** Where are spores formed (i) on the fern plant, and (ii) on a moss plant?

(b) Mosses and ferns produce flask-shaped female sex organs. Where are these formed on (i) mosses, and (ii) ferns?

(c) List the labels indicated on the drawing of a part of a moss plant, *Funaria*, and part of a fern plant, *Dryopteris*.

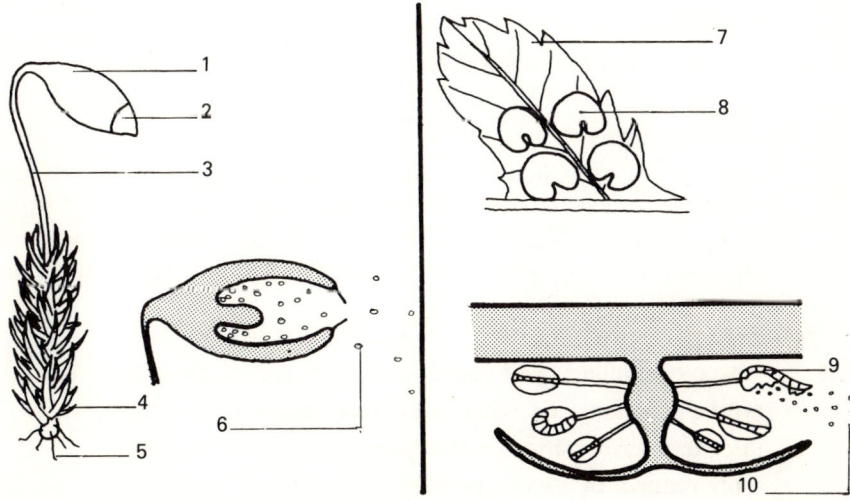

39.3 **(a)** State TWO important biological ways in which the pine tree differs from a flowering tree.

[(b)] Large areas of mountain side and moorland are planted with coniferous trees in the wetter regions of the United Kingdom.

(i) Why do conifers benefit from wetter conditions?

(ii) Why are conifers a useful or valuable crop for a land-owner to plant?

(iii) Coniferous woodlands have been described almost as deserts. Suggest reasons why other plants and animals are absent from coniferous woods.

40 Single-celled (acellular) animals; *Amoeba*

40.1 Animals without backbones (the invertebrates) include the structurally simple animals made of one cell only.

(a) What are one-celled animals called?

(b) Some of the animals move by flowing, but others move differently. State one other mechanism of movement adopted by single-celled animals.

(c) Where does *Amoeba* occur naturally?

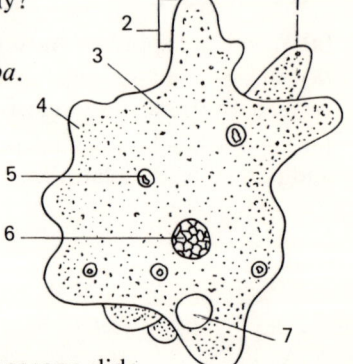

40.2 (a) List the labels on the active *Amoeba*.

(b) Explain briefly how *Amoeba*:

(i) obtains oxygen

(ii) excretes carbon dioxide

(iii) excretes water

(iv) takes in food (e.g. a ciliate)

(v) obtains nitrogen

(vi) gets rid of undigested food

(vii) moves over the surface of a microscope slide

(viii) reproduces.

(c) If the mineral salt content of the water around an *Amoeba* is very slowly increased, which activity of the cell would you expect to slow down first?

(d) Living amoebae and green flagellates are present in a dish which is illuminated at one end only. If amoebae tend to accumulate at the illuminated end, what conclusion would you draw?

40.3 Give ONE similarity and ONE difference in each of the following:

(a) the process of digestion in *Amoeba* and in a mammal

(b) external respiration of *Amoeba* and a fish

(c) movement of *Amoeba* and *Hydra*.

41 Coelenterates; *Hydra*

41.1 List the labels to the parts indicated in the drawing of *Hydra*

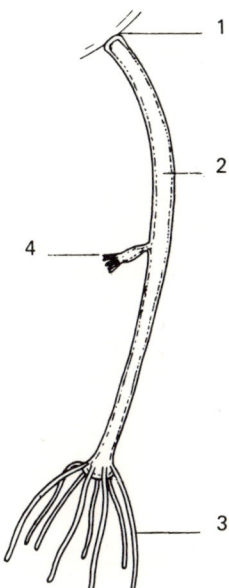

41.2 Copy the table and complete it by giving ONE important difference between *Hydra* and the organism listed in column 1, for the feature given in column 2.

COLUMN 1	COLUMN 2	DIFFERENCE FOUND IN *HYDRA*
earthworm	structure of food canal	
sundew	capture of prey	
Amoeba	digestion	
Amoeba	egestion	
earthworm	contraction	
mammal	reproduction	
fish	intake of oxygen	
Chlamydomonas (or *Euglena*)	movement	

41.3 (a) Hydras were found living in an aquarium of pond water which appeared to have no *Daphnia* present. How do the Hydras obtain food and survive in these circumstances?

(b) How does a hungry *Hydra* exploit its environment for food?

(c) State briefly how you would test whether *Hydra* is sensitive to light.

82 Parasitic worms/Segmented worms

41.4 (a) What is the difference in symmetry of *Hydra* and an earthworm?

(b) Using *Hydra* as ONE example, give THREE biological uses of the words 'bud' or 'budding'.

42 Parasitic worms; *Taenia*

42.1 An example of an animal parasite is the pork tapeworm (*Taenia solium*).

(a) Explain why pork tapeworms are now rarely found in the UK.

(b) How does a tapeworm increase in numbers?

(c) Which is the primary host of *Taenia* and which is the secondary?

(d) (i) How does *Taenia* get from each of the hosts to the other?

(ii) What is its final destination in each host?

(e) How is the adult tapeworm attached to its host? Make a sketch to illustrate your answer.

43 Segmented worms; *Lumbricus* (Earthworm)

43.1 Soil is a mixture of mineral particles, organic matter, air and water, and it supports an enormous population of micro-organisms and small animals.

(a) List FOUR ways in which earthworms improve the quality of soil.

(b) How would you attempt to estimate the number of earthworms in an area of land?

(c) How does an earthworm take in food?

(d) Is the time of feeding on the soil surface important? Give a reason.

(e) What visible evidence generally indicates that an earthworm has been collecting food?

43.2 (a) Why is the earthworm described as a segmented worm?

(b) Make a list of the labels of the structures indicated on the drawing of the earthworm at the top of the next page.

(c) What type of symmetry occurs in this animal?

43.3 (a) When an earthworm moves on smooth paper in the laboratory there is a scratching noise and a slimy trail left. Suggest an explanation for this observation, and of what significance it is in the movement of the earthworm through the soil.

(b) Make labelled drawings to show the sequence of changes in shape that occur in the earthworm's body during movement.

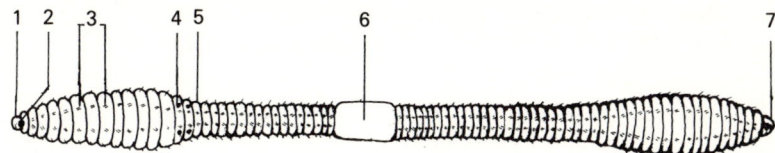

The earthworm-ventral view

43.4 The earthworm is hermaphrodite.
(a) What does 'hermaphrodite' mean?
(b) How is self-fertilization avoided?

44 Insects

44.1 Label the external features indicated in the drawings of a honey bee and a cockroach.

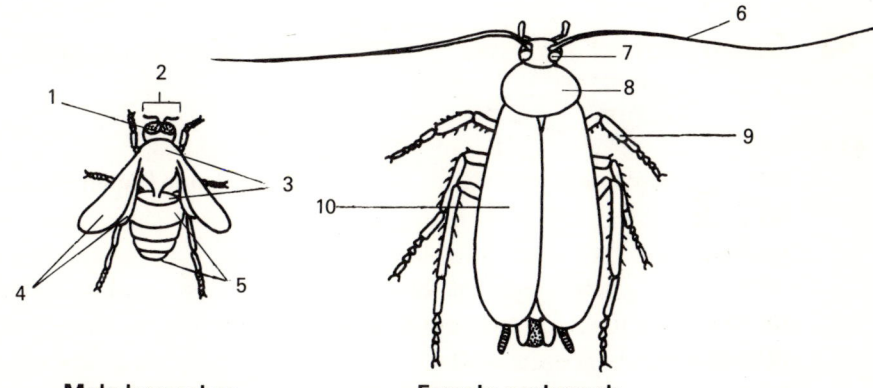

Male honey bee   Female cockroach

44.2 Copy and complete the following schemes to show two distinct patterns of insect life history. Add the name of one more example of each type.

(a) Adult ——— Egg

.... ——— ....
Examples, butterfly and ....

(b) Adult ——— Egg

.... ——— ....
Examples, cockroach and ....

44.3 (a) Mouthparts of insects differ in various species. Give examples of THREE distinct types of feeding mouthparts.

(b) Not all insects have two pairs of wings. Name TWO insects that do not have two pairs and suggest what modification has occurred.

44.4 Examine the scheme for the life-history of the large cabbage white butterfly, showing the approximate timings.

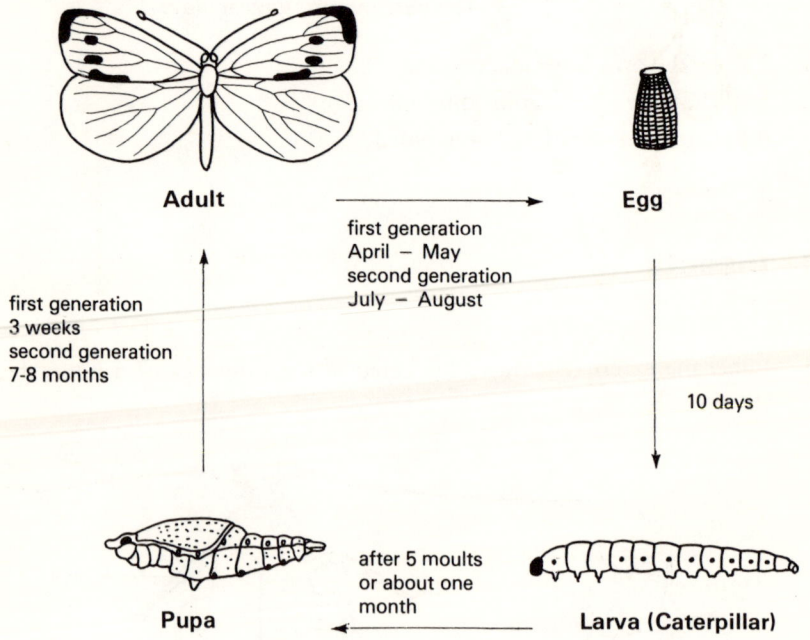

(a) When and where would you look for eggs of a cabbage white butterfly?
(b) When does moulting (ecdysis) occur in the life-history of butterflies?
(c) Why is moulting necessary?
(d) In what form and where does this insect survive the winter?
(e) When do the wings of a butterfly form?
(f) When do the newly-exposed wings expand?
(g) What causes the expansion of butterflies' wings?
(h) How is exchange of gases achieved in insects for the purpose of respiration?

44.5 Examine the drawing opposite of larva and adult bees in the life history of the honey bee, and note the approximate times between the stages indicated.
(a) If a major misfortune overtakes the majority of foraging bees of a hive, how many days will elapse before the queen bee can significantly increase the total number of adult worker bees available in the colony?

(b) Give ONE difference for each of the following pairs:
  (i) food of a queen larva, and a worker larva
  (ii) cell of a queen larva, and a worker larva
  (iii) eggs hatching into a male larva, and a female larva
  (iv) nectar and honey.
(c) How does a bee know that another bee is from a different colony?
(d) What is collected by bees for food?
(e) Only a few bees ('scouts') search for food, as distinct from collecting it. How does a bee *collecting* food know where to find a new supply?
(f) How is the structure of a worker's body related to:
  (i) its function of food collecting
  (ii) building honeycombs
  (iii) guarding the hive entrance?
(g) Give TWO reasons why the honey bee is a good pollinator of flowers which it visits.

44.6 (a) Where and on what does the adult housefly feed?
  (b) Name THREE diseases that may be spread by the housefly.
  (c) In what different ways does the adult housefly carry disease?
  (d) State THREE distinct methods of reducing the spread of these diseases.

44.7 (a) How could you test whether a captured housefly is carrying bacteria?

(b) What control would you set up at the same time?

44.8 Where does the female adult mosquito (a) lay its eggs, and (b) feed? Give details of this process.

44.9 (a) Where do mosquito larvae live and feed?

(b) How does the mosquito larva obtain oxygen?

44.10 (a) State a disease that an adult mosquito transmits.

(b) Why is it necessary to make only cautious use of the insecticides that effectively kill the adult mosquitoes?

(c) From our knowledge of the complete life-cycle of the mosquito, what other ways of controlling mosquitoes are available?

45 Fish

45.1 (a) List the external features of the stickleback indicated on the diagram.

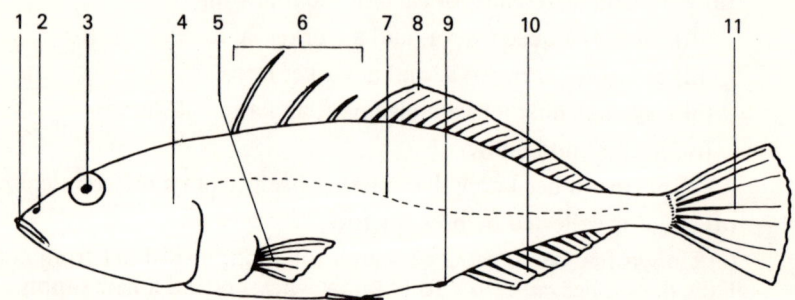

(b) What features may be interpreted as adaptations to life in water?

45.2 (a) Copy the diagram of the dorsal view of the dogfish. Annotate your drawing to show how the fish moves forward in the water.

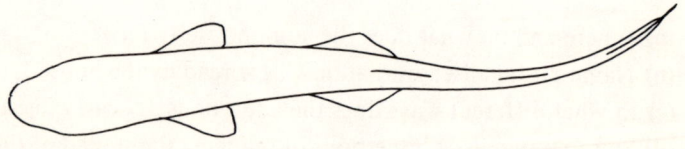

(b) What structures of the fish help to prevent: (i) roll, (ii) pitch, and (iii) yaw of the body in the water?

(c) Give TWO differences between cartilaginous and bony fish, and name ONE example of each.

45.3 Give the names of three sense organs possessed by most fish and the use made of them.

45.4 (a) Explain briefly by means of your own annotated diagram how exchange of oxygen and carbon dioxide occurs in fish.

(b) Why does a fish that preys on smaller fish not chew its food?

46 Amphibia; the frog

46.1 (a) List the external features of the frog indicated on the diagram.

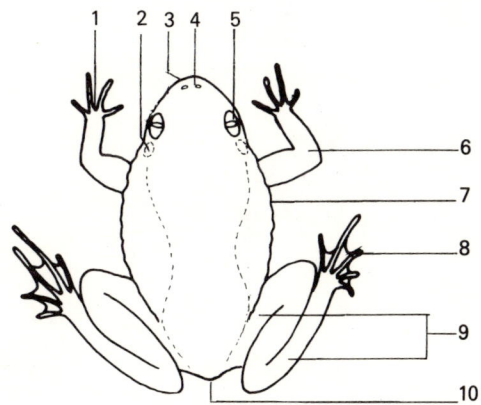

(b) In what way does the skin of the frog differ from that of the fish?

46.2 How does a frog capture its prey?

46.3 (a) A frog may show rapid repeated muscular activity of the buccal cavity. Of what value is this?

(b) Periodically, this rapid movement is replaced by a single slower movement. What is this and of what value is it to the frog?

(c) At times, no movement (of the two types mentioned) appears to occur. Give an explanation of this.

46.4 (a) A pair of frogs produce many tadpoles. Why do the numbers of adult frogs not increase rapidly?

(b) Name THREE common predators of tadpoles.

46.5 Below are drawn tadpoles at two different stages. At each stage describe how the tadpole (i) obtains nutrients, and (ii) obtains oxygen.

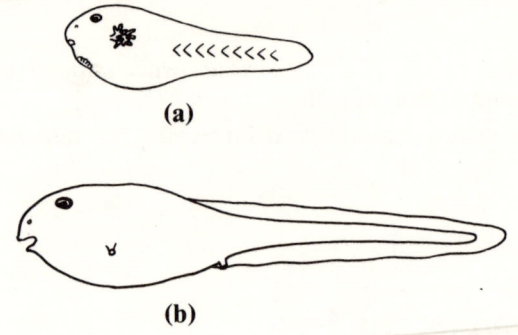

47 Birds

47.1 (a) List the external features of a bird of prey indicated on the diagram below.

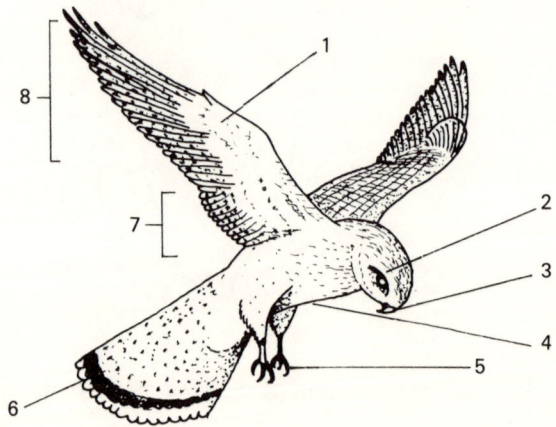

(b) For each of the following give ONE way in which the feathers of birds:
  (i) aid flight
  (ii) aid landing at the end of a flight
  (iii) maintain body temperature
  (iv) change in appearance during one year.

(c) Why does a bird, sleeping on a perch, not fall off?

47.2 (a) Make a large labelled drawing to show the position of the air-sacs in relation to the lungs in the body of the bird.

(b) Give two advantages which may be attributed to the system of air-sacs in a pigeon.

47.3 (a) Explain why fertilization in a bird must be in the upper oviduct.

(b) List the structures indicated in the drawing of a bird's egg.

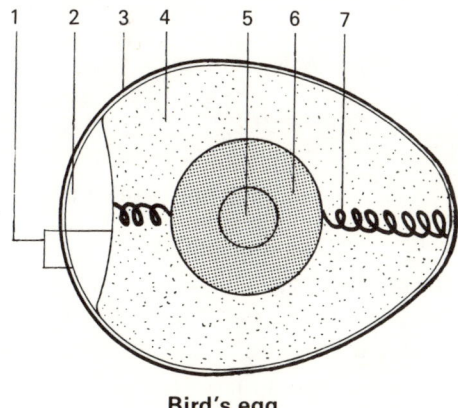

Bird's egg

47.4 State the useful consequence to birds of eating grit.

48 Mammals

48.1 (a) Give FIVE characteristics of mammals not found in any other organism.

(b) (i) Name a characteristic of mammals found in all birds but not in any other organism.

(ii) What characteristic is rare in mammals but found in all birds?

(c) How do marsupials differ from other mammals?

48.2 (a) What do you understand by the term 'pentadactyl limb'?

(b) State what particular limb structures have developed in named mammals which specialize in:

(i) flight

(ii) swimming

(iii) scratching and digging

(iv) running fast.

49 Parasitism, mutualism (symbiosis) and commensalism

49.1 In the lichen association, fungal cells and simple green plant cells (algae) live together for mutual benefit.

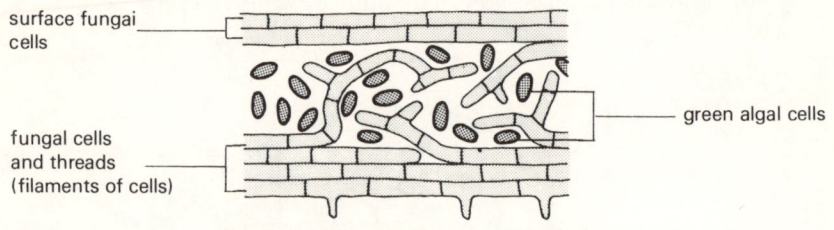

Section through lichen plant body

(a) What is this type of relationship called?

(b) Lichens occur on many surfaces, often well above ground. What advantage may the algal cells gain from the association?

(c) What benefit may the algal cells provide the fungus?

(d) Lichens rarely occur close to large towns and few species occur in cities. What explanation can you offer for this?

49.2 (a) Give ONE characteristic which both plant and animal parasites generally have in common.

(b) Distinguish between ectoparasites and endoparasites of animals.

(c) How does the adult tapeworm feed and obtain a balanced diet?

(d) Mistletoe is a green plant with leaves, and grows 'rooted' in the branches of host trees. Describe the nutrition of mistletoe.

49.3 Dodder is a plant parasite that lives on nettle and other host plants.

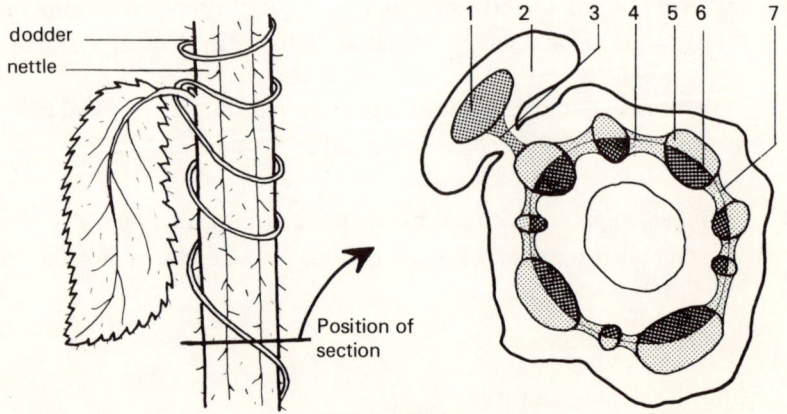

Dodder growing on nettle stem

(a) List the parts indicated, in the section of dodder and host.

(b) How does dodder become established on host plants from seeds produced in the previous year?

49.4 Root nodules occur on the roots of members of the pea family (leguminous plants).

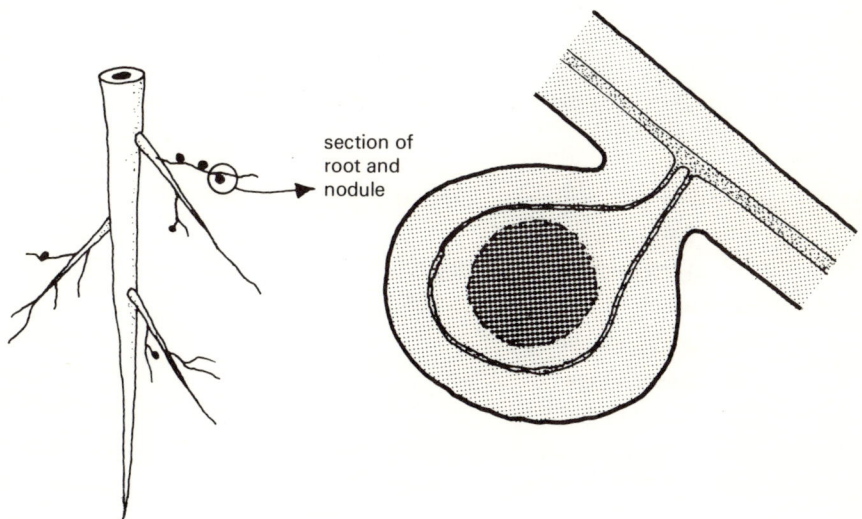

Root nodules on roots of a leguminous plant

(a) Copy the diagram of the section of a nodule and root, label it, and annotate your drawing to show the site of the nodule occupants and the pathway of transport of materials between both partners of the nodule.

(b) What benefit do you think both partners gain?

(c) Why is clover seed usually included with grass seed when a field of grass is sown?

(d) Crops like wheat and barley are often treated with nitrates in the spring, but meadows with clover are not. Why is this?

[49.5] Commensalism is a relationship between two organisms where one partner is neither harmed nor helped but the other partner derives some benefit. Classify the following associations as parasitic, mutualistic, or commensal, stating why.

(a) Nectar-sucking insects and the flowers they visit.

(b) Aphids living and feeding on bean stems.

(c) Large sharks and the pilot fish shoals that swim nearby.

(d) The population of bacteria in the human gut.

(e) The fruiting fungi with fungal threads forming a tight mantle around the roots of forest trees (mycorrhiza).

(f) Spangle gall larvae in the galls on the undersurface of oak leaves.

50 Saprophytic organisms; the cycling of carbon and nitrogen in nature

50.1 (a) How do saprophytes differ from parasites in their nutrition?

(b) Why does a heap of fresh lawn mowings heat up?

(c) Outline two different ways in which the saprophytic nutrition of yeast is used by man in food and drink production.

(d) Which two types of saprophytic organisms are involved in the production of 'blue' cheese?

50.2 (a) Bacteria are commonly found in the soil. Why are soil bacteria important to most plants?

(b) What part is played by bacteria in the following:
   (i) making butter
   (ii) making vinegar
   (iii) making silage
   (iv) making linen?

(c) Since silage and compost are both produced from cut grass, how does the farmer control bacterial action in the silage clamp to prevent decay to compost?

50.3 The diagram below is a simplified summary of the nitrogen cycle.

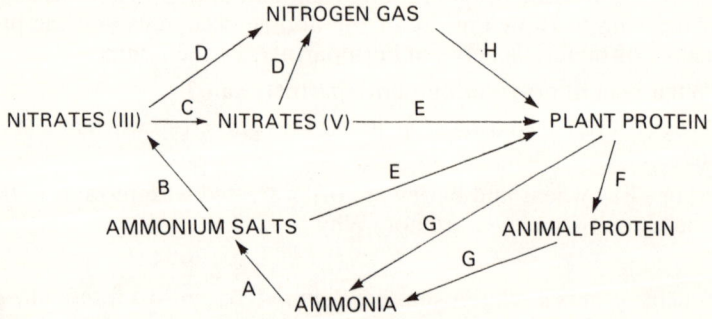

(a) How is plant protein converted into animal protein (stage F)?

(b) Where does nitrogen gas occur naturally?

(c) Name one organism that assists in the conversion of nitrogen gas into plant protein. Where would you find this organism growing? (stage H)

(d) By what process does protein in living things become ammonia (stage G), and what organisms are involved in this conversion?

(e) State one site of protein manufacture in (i) a green plant, and (ii) a mammal.

(f) How are nitrates and ammonium salts absorbed by green plants (stage E)?

(g) Under what conditions do soil organisms convert soil nitrates to nitrogen gas (stage D)?

(h) How are ammonium salts converted to nitrates in the soil and by what organisms (stage B and C)?

[50.4] The drawing represents a scene in winter. Name FOUR processes, each directly connected with the nitrogen cycle, which are slowed down in winter, and TWO processes which carry on at the same rate.

50.5 Carbon is present in all organic compounds and in carbon dioxide gas in the atmosphere.
(a) In what processes will carbon of organic compounds be converted to carbon of carbon dioxide?
(b) When does conversion from carbon dioxide to organic compounds occur?

50.6 **(a)** Describe a part played by bacteria in the carbon cycle.
(b) In which processes (in the carbon cycle) is energy (i) used, (ii) released?

50.7 Trace a carbon 'chain' from the atmosphere to carbon in **(a)** paper, **(b)** glycogen.

[50.8] **(a)** Design an experiment to test whether carbon is present in matchsticks.
(b) What precaution can be taken in your experiment to ensure that the carbon can only have come from the matchsticks?

[50.9] What part in the carbon cycle is played by the oceans and organisms in them?

51 Ecology; man and the environment

51.1 Which of the following statements is a correct definition of ecology?
A Study of the developing shortage of fossil fuel and of the steps being taken to conserve fuel stocks.
B Study of plants and animals in their natural surroundings.
C Study of the naming of plants and animals and of their classification in related families.
D Study of the problems created by pollution of the natural environment by the actions of man.

51.2 Below are organisms of a simple food web.

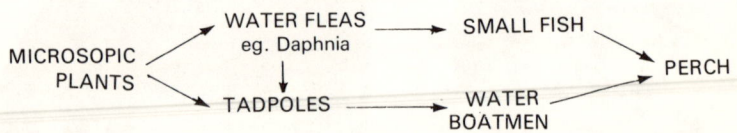

(a) In what habitat would you expect to find these organisms?
(b) What particular pieces of apparatus or equipment would you need to take with you in the field to collect samples of these organisms in order to observe in the laboratory.
(c) What is the difference between a food chain and a food web?
(d) What is the ultimate energy source of the food web shown here?
(e) From the food web given here write the name of an organism fitting each of the following categories:
   (i) plant
   (ii) herbivore
   (iii) carnivore
   (iv) omnivore.
(f) From the food web given here write the name of one organism fitting each of the following categories:
   (i) primary producer
   (ii) primary consumer
   (iii) secondary consumer
   (iv) tertiary consumer.

51.3 A chemical is a pollutant when its presence in the environment is harmful to living things. The burning of fossil fuel generates carbon dioxide, dust, and sulphur dioxide.
(a) Why is carbon dioxide not classed as a pollutant to green plants?
(b) In what ways is sulphur dioxide harmful to living things?

(c) In what ways is dust harmful (i) to plants, and (ii) to mammals?

(d) Many petrol fuels, when burnt, release lead compounds into the air. In what ways are lead and its compounds harmful to living things?

51.4 Food chains can be expressed as pyramids of numbers showing a reduction in numbers of organisms from the producer at the base to the consumer at the top.

(a) In an investigation of a woodland which of the following pyramids would you expect?

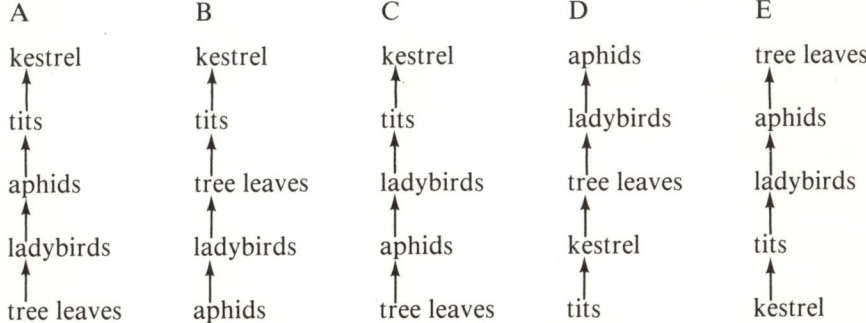

(b) What is the primary source of energy in all food chains?

[51.5] (a) Properly treated sewage causes no problem for rivers into which the effluent is discharged. Raw (untreated) sewage that is drained directly into a river causes the death of fish and other large animals a little down river. What is the main biological cause of death of the fish?

(b) If an excess of fertilizer is drained or washed down into a pond or lake the death of fish and other large animals occurs a little while later. What is the main biological cause of death of the fish?

(c) Nitrates from fertilizers are increasingly polluting drinking water taken from lakes and rivers. Why are excessive quantities of nitrates particularly harmful to babies fed on milk made up or diluted with tap water?

[51.6] Crop rotation involves changing what is grown on a particular field from year to year by a programme of rotating crops through a four- or five-year cycle.

(a) State two distinct hazards of growing the same crop on land year after year.

(b) (i) Outline an appropriate scheme of rotation.

(ii) How would this scheme actually improve the soil?

(c) What is the advantage to the soil and soil structure of applying:

(i) farmyard manure

(ii) artificial manure?

(d) Crop-rotation programmes have not been practised universally in the presence of cheap and readily-available chemical pesticides. For ONE named pesticide, state the advantages and disadvantages its use brings.

52 Health and disease; food preservation

52.1 (a) Give TWO differences between a bacterium and a virus.

(b) Name (i) TWO human diseases caused by bacteria, (ii) TWO human diseases caused by viruses, (iii) TWO human diseases caused by neither bacteria nor viruses.

[52.2] Some mature (drying) grass leaves are gently boiled for about a minute in sterilized milk, to try to isolate spore-forming bacteria.
(a) What does boiling do to active bacteria?

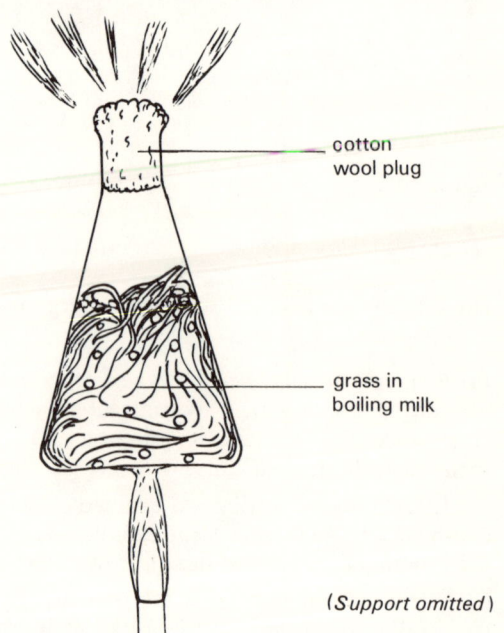

(*Support omitted*)

Experiment

(b) What does boiling do to bacterial spores?

(c) What is the point of using milk?

(d) Why is the boiling done with a cotton-wool plug inserted?

(e) How can one tell whether live bacteria are present a few days later without removing any of the contents of the flask?

[52.3] (a) State THREE ways in which disease 'germs' enter the body.

(b) For each of these state ONE different means of defence by the body.

52.4 (a) What is the source and mode of action of (i) white blood cells, and (ii) antibodies?

(b) Distinguish between natural and artificially-acquired immunity.

(c) Would it be beneficial if for a time we made no contact with disease germs? Give a reason.

52.5 (a) Give TWO reasons why canned (tinned) food does not usually deteriorate.

(b) A bowl of soup and a dish of jam are left uncovered on a shelf in midsummer. Explain which you expect to deteriorate first, giving your reasons.

(c) In hot countries, fish and meat may be dried in the sun and sold. Why should these keep much longer than untreated fish and meat?

(d) Why does cooking food help to preserve it?

(e) Explain why the following should keep well in a larder: (i) pickled onions, (ii) biscuits, (iii) cured bacon, (iv) sultanas, (v) sugar.

(f) How does a refrigerator help in food preservation?

52.6 (a) What is pasteurized milk?

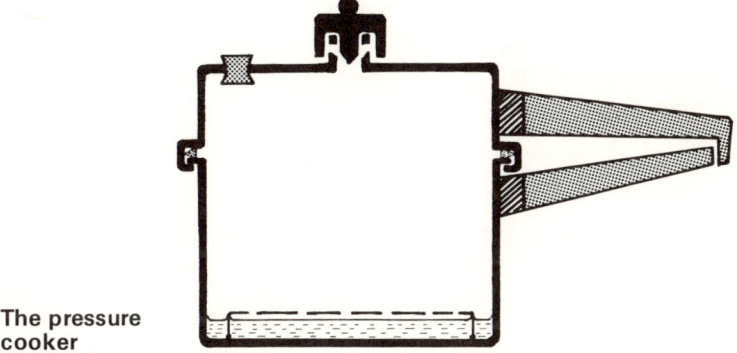

The pressure cooker

(b) The pressure cooker can be used to cook rapidly and to sterilize food (or equipment, apparatus and media). Copy the diagram and annotate your drawing of the pressure cooker to explain how it is used and how it works.

53 Genetics

53.1 Gregor Mendel carried out breeding experiments with garden pea plants, publishing his results in 1865. In one of these experiments pure-breeding pea plants which had grown from smooth-coated seeds were crossed with plants from seeds with wrinkled seed coats, and all the seeds produced were found to have smooth coats. These seeds and the plants that grew from them were called the first filial generation, or F_1 generation. When he grew plants from these seeds and allowed them to self-pollinate he found this second generation (F_2) of pea seeds were 893 with smooth coats and 298 with wrinkled coats.

(a) In Mendel's explanation of his results he used the term 'factor'. What is our term for 'factors' and where in the cell do they occur?

98   Genetics

(b) The parent plants have diploid cells, the gametes are haploid. What do we mean by haploid and diploid? Where do male and female gametes occur in the pea plant?

(c) By reference to Mendel's experiment described above, define the following terms and give an example of each:

    (i) homozygous and heterozygous

    (ii) dominant and recessive

    (iii) genotype and phenotype.

(d) For the F_2 generation why were the results obtained not three smooth-coated peas to each one wrinkled-coated pea?

(e) If some of the F_1 generation were crossed with pure-breeding smooth plants, show (i) what types of gametes would be formed, and (ii) what the resulting offspring will be.

53.2 Copy and complete the schemes given to answer each part of the question. In the fruit fly, brown eye colour is recessive to red eye colour.

(a) Show clearly the phenotype and the genotype of a brown-eyed fly and a heterozygous red-eyed fly. (Use the symbol R to represent the gene giving red eye colour.)

    PHENOTYPE   ....

    GENOTYPE   ....

(b) If these two kinds are bred together, what eye colours appear in the offspring and in what proportion?

    GAMETES   ....

    F_1 (genotypes)   ....

    F_1 PHENOTYPES   ....

    Percentage of red-eyed flies =

    Percentage of brown-eyed flies =

(c) If the heterozygous flies are inbred what percentage of offspring are brown-eyed?

    PHENOTYPE   ....

    GENOTYPE   ....

    GAMETES   ....

    F_1 (genotypes)   ....

    F_1 PHENOTYPES   ....

    Percentage of brown-eyed flies =

53.3 You are given three seeds which vary in size and weight, but you learn that they were obtained from a single plant. How would you test whether the variation is heritable or non-heritable?

53.4 (a) The features given below were studied in a class of school-children. Which are in fact continuous variations and which discontinuous variations?

   (i) height
   (ii) weight
   (iii) colour of hair
   (iv) ability to taste phenylthiocarbamide (PTC)
   (v) pulse rate
   (vi) type of fingerprint.

(b) Give ONE example of each of the following:

   (i) a heritable variation (characteristic) not normally affected by the environment
   (ii) a heritable variation (characteristic) which can be affected by the environment
   (iii) a non-heritable variation (characteristic) occurring in an animal
   (iv) a non-heritable variation (characteristic) occurring in a plant.

53.5 (a) What difference would you expect to see with a microscope in squash preparations of chromosomes of men and women?

(b) What is the difference in origin of fraternal and identical twins?

53.6 Cattle of coat of chestnut brown mixed with white (roan cattle) are produced by crossing homozygous red and homozygous white cattle. Using the symbol R (for gene producing red coat) copy and complete the following scheme to show the colour of coat in the F_2 generation.

Parent phenotype	red coat	white coat
Parent genotype	....	....
Parent gametes	....	....
F_1	.... (100% roan)	
F_1 gametes	...... and .... crossed with .... and	
F_2 genotypes	....	
F_2 phenotypes	....	
Proportion:	....	

53.7 In mice, black fur is dominant to chocolate-coloured fur, so that if a homozygous black mouse is crossed with a chocolate one, in the F_1 generation the progeny will be all black, but when these animals are crossed there will be approximately three black mice to every chocolate one, in the F_2 generation.

Show how a cross with a recessive helps in discovering the genotypes of the F_2 black mice.

[53.8] The disease of haemophilia is genetically controlled, and the gene concerned is a recessive one, and is carried on the X chromosome in the terminal position. In the following human pedigree

○   represents a normal female, genotype $X_H X_H$
◐   represents a carrier female, genotype $X_H X_h$ (she is not haemophiliac)
□   represents a normal male, genotype $X_H Y$
■   represents a haemophiliac male, genotype $X_h Y$.

Human pedigree for the incidence of haemophilia in a family:

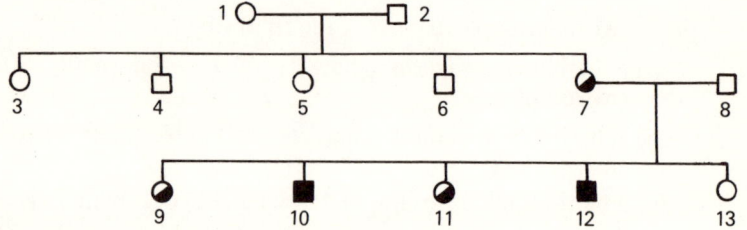

(a) What are the genotypes for persons 1 and 2?
(b) What form does the disease of haemophilia take?
(c) Why are there no female adults with a genotype $X_h X_h$?
(d) What are the genotypes of persons 7 and 8?
(e) What is a mutation?
(f) Is there evidence for a mutation in either persons 1 or 2?
(g) If person 10 married a normal female and they had only male children would any of these children be haemophiliac? Give a reason.

54 Evolution; the work of Darwin

54.1   Vast numbers of (1) of animals and plants are living today, and for many years biologists have been interested in how such (2) has come into existence. The biologist most associated with this issue is (3). As a student at University he was a (4), and in 1832 he became the ship's naturalist on (5) that was to make a map-making survey (6). The voyage lasted almost 5 years, and on long stops at places such as the (7) there was an excellent opportunity to study the flora and fauna of (8) and local communities. Subsequent to this long voyage he worked at his home, consolidating his evidence for (9) and worked out a plausible hypothesis for the (10). After 20 years of this study he published a (11) with co-author (12), entitled *A Theory of Evolution by Natural Selection*. A year later he published (13) *On the Origin of Species by Natural Selection*, the first account of a theory that was supported by (14).

Write down the numbers 1–14 representing the gaps in the passage at the base of the previous page. Select the most appropriate word or words from the list below to correctly complete the following account of the work of Darwin.

(a) similar species
(b) different species
(c) diversity of life
(d) Charles Darwin
(e) Thomas Huxley
(f) Alfred Wallace
(g) J.B. Lamarck
(h) keen naturalist
(i) ships physician
(j) HMS Beagle
(k) around the world
(l) to America and the West Indies
(m) Galapagos Islands
(n) isolated
(o) connected
(p) fact of evolution
(q) mechanism of evolution
(r) special creation of species
(s) acquired characteristics
(t) short paper
(u) newspaper article
(v) his book
(w) evidence in detail
(x) public discussion.

[54.2] Which of the following statements are correct concerning the theory of natural selection?

A All living things of the same species differ from each other in many ways. Variation is a characteristic of life.

B The actual numbers of living things mostly stay fairly constant over long periods, yet young are usually produced at a rate sufficient to double the numbers with each generation.

C There is a struggle for existence amongst members of a population, and many fail to survive.

D The differences between individuals give some organisms an advantage in the struggle for existence. Natural selection of some variations occurs, and results in the survival of the fittest.

E When organisms survive and reproduce they pass on their characteristics, including successful variations, to their off-spring.

F Natural selection is a process that causes variations to arise in individuals.

For any incorrect statement rewrite it as a fully correct statement.

54.3 (a) What is the difference between natural and artificial selection?

(b) What part may mutations play in the origin of heritable variations?

55 Biological illustrations: an exercise in observation, identification and interpretation

55.1

Shell International Petrol Co plc

(a) What stage in the life-cycle of the cabbage white butterfly is this?
(b) Where is this structure to be found in nature?
(c) What features suggest to you that this is a stationary phase in the life-cycle?
(d) What changes occur inside this structure? State in general how such changes are controlled and co-ordinated.

55.2 (a) Which region of a plant root has been sectioned to show this structure?
(b) List appropriate labels for 1 – 3.
(c) Where and how does the root take in nitrate ions and oxygen?

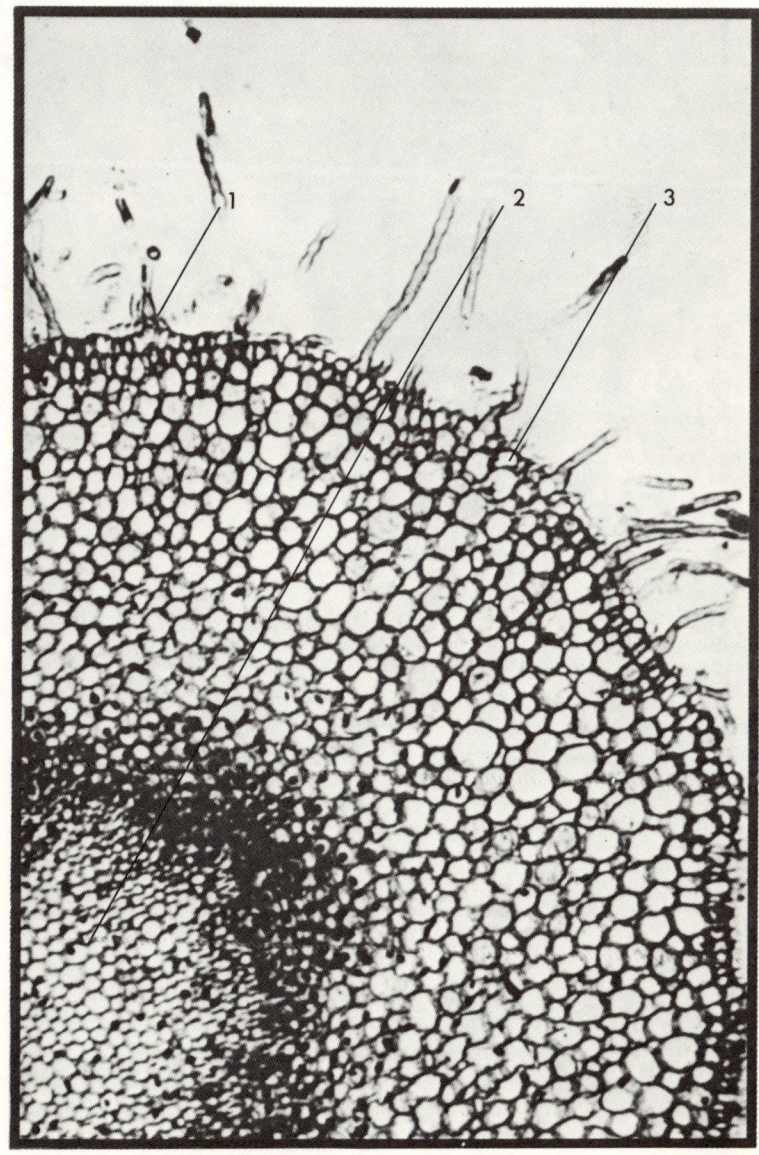

Gene Cox

104 Biological illustrations

55.3

Radio Times Hulton Pict Lib

(a) What feature unique to mammals do these children exhibit?
(b) What disease does the child on the right have?
(c) What has caused the disease, and how can it be prevented?
(d) What is the difference between this disease and scurvy that sailors used to get on long voyages?

55.4

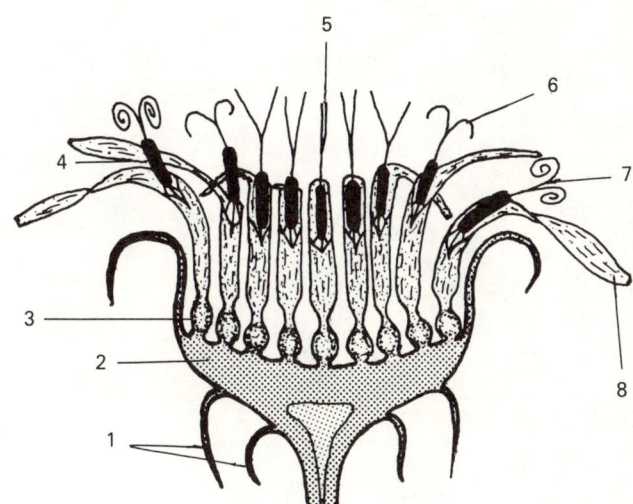

Chris Clegg

(a) Is this structure a solitary flower? To what family does it belong?
(b) List the structures 1–8.
(c) How is pollination achieved and assured in this plant?
(d) This plant produces fruit. What do they look like and how are they dispersed?

55.5

Howard Jay

(a) What external features indicate that this animal is an insect?
(b) List the structures 1–7.
(c) Where and how does this animal feed?
(d) What problems of structure and function arise for insects with large bodies (or, in effect, why are there no really large insects)?

55.6

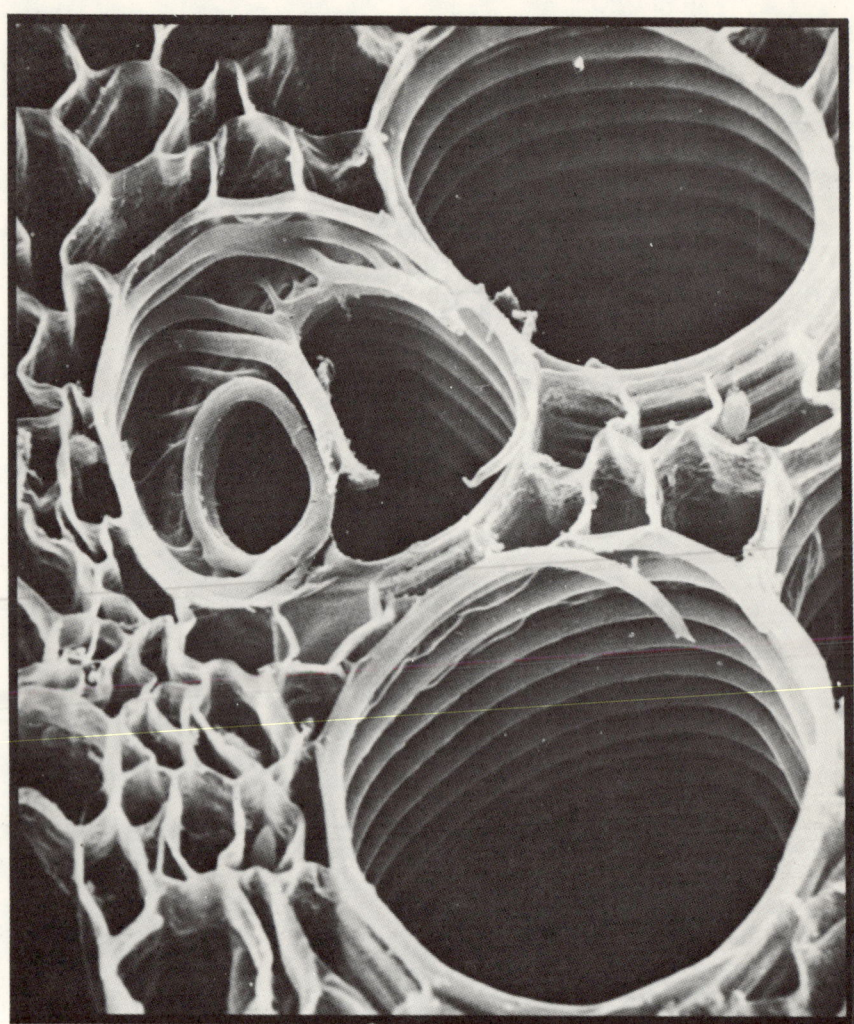

Dr Richard Johnson

(a) The large tubes were observed in a plant leaf stalk. What substances pass along them?
(b) Spirally arranged thickenings occur on the inner surfaces of the tubes. What does their presence prevent?
(c) What substances make up the walls?
(d) How can water inside the tube get out into surrounding cells?

55.7

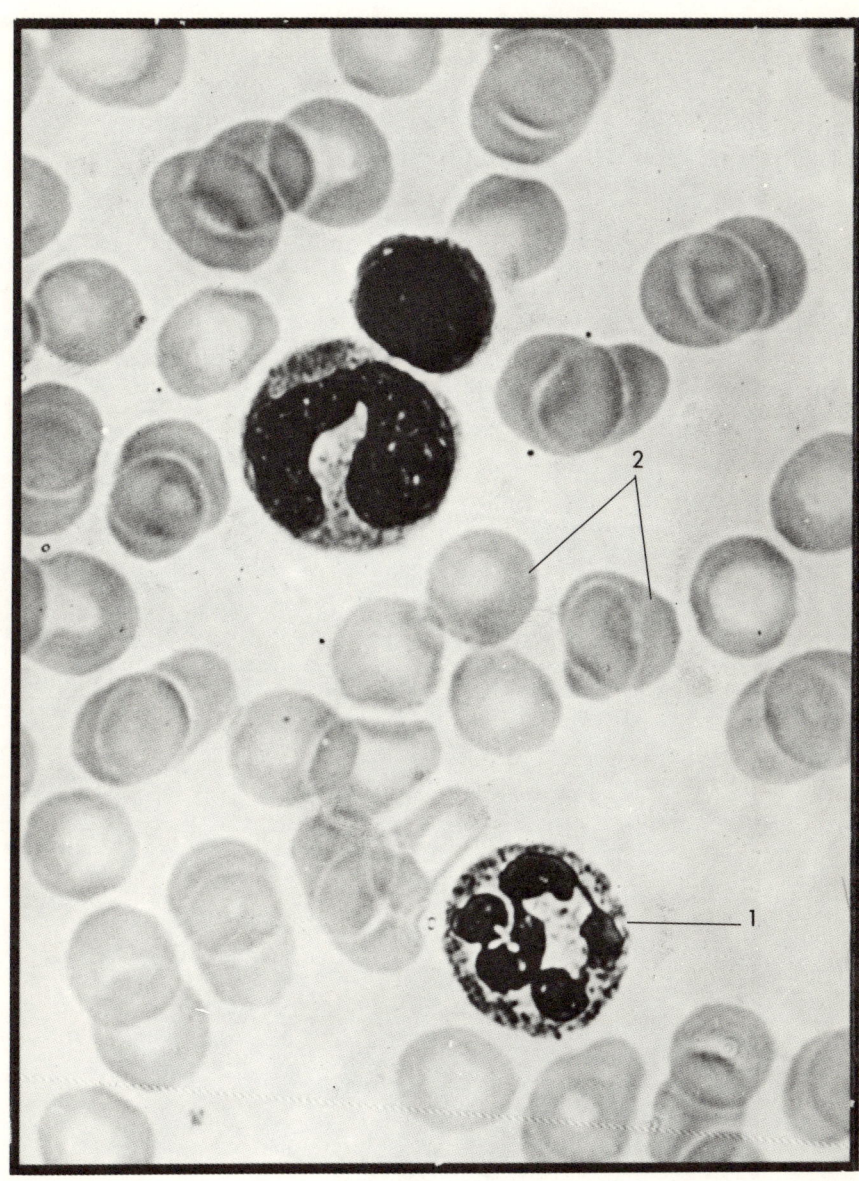

Gene Cox

(a) List the names of the cells indicated 1 and 2.
(b) What role does cell 1 play in the life of a mammal?
(c) What role does cell 2 play in the life of a mammal?
(d) Name a parasite that feeds on mammal's blood.
(e) Where are 1-type cells made in the body, and where are 2-type cells destroyed in the body?

55.8

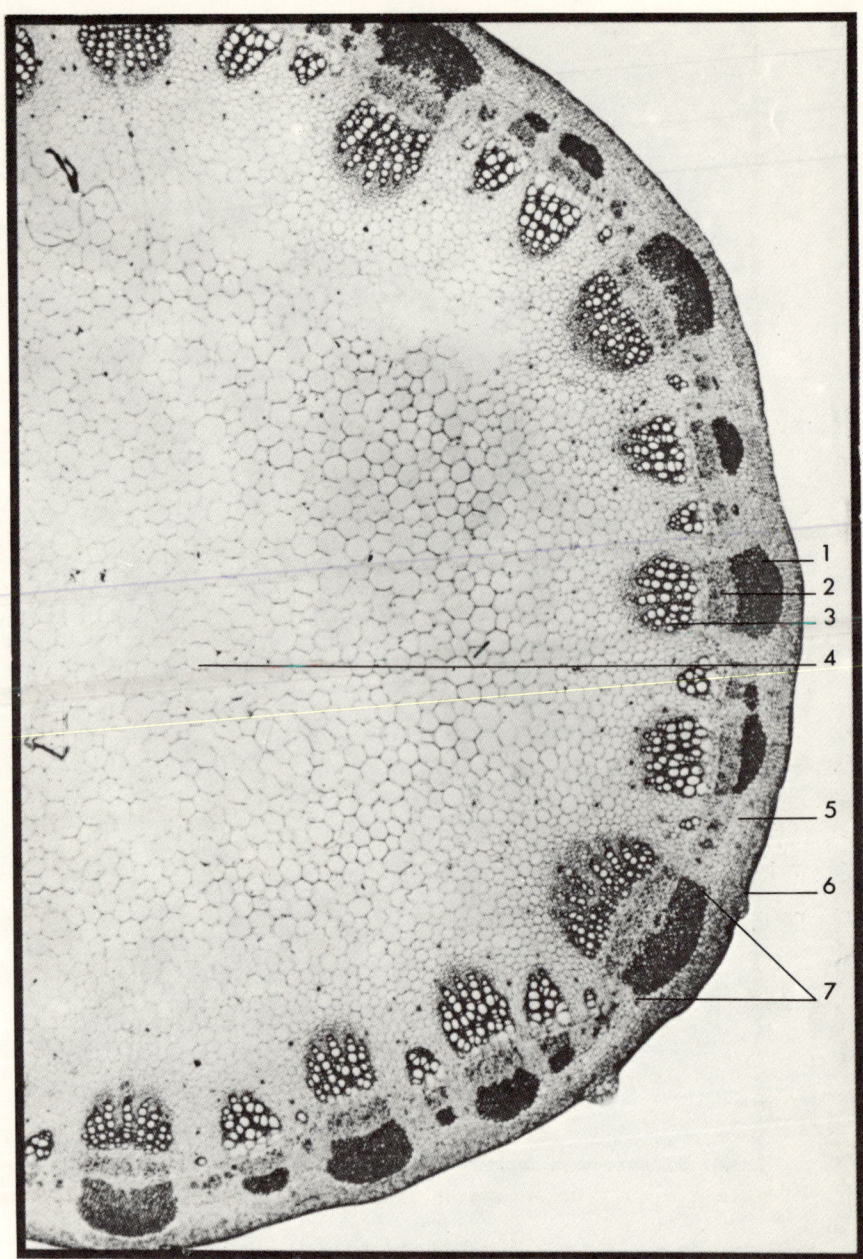

Gene Cox

(a) Is this TS of a stem, or of a root?
(b) List the structures 1 – 7.
(c) What part do the vascular bundles play in the transport of foods, and in the support of the whole structure?
(d) How does water move from cells of the cortex to cells of the pith?

55.9

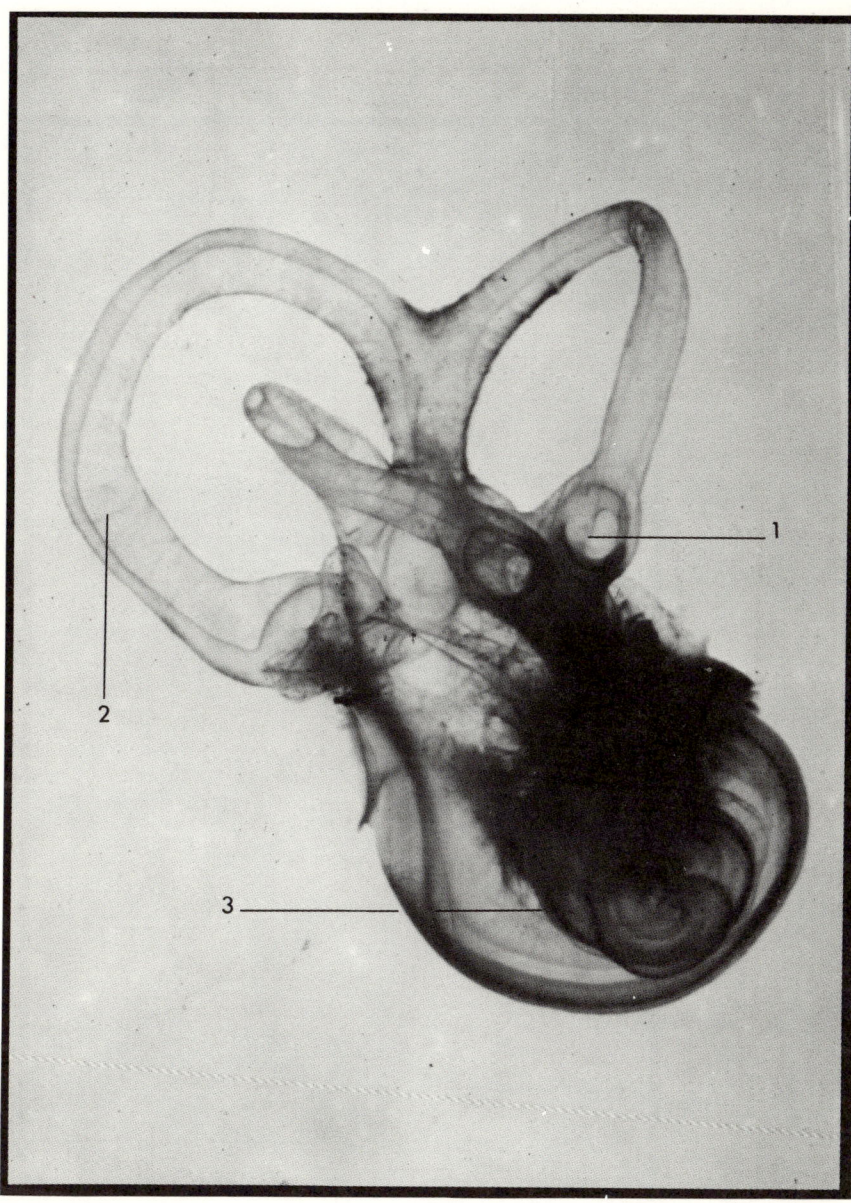

From *Revised Nuffield Biology* (1975) Longman

(a) Where does this structure occur in the mammal's body?
(b) What is it surrounded by in the body?
(c) What parts of the brain do nerves connect it to?
(d) List the structures 1 – 3.
(e) What is the function of 2 and 3?

55.10

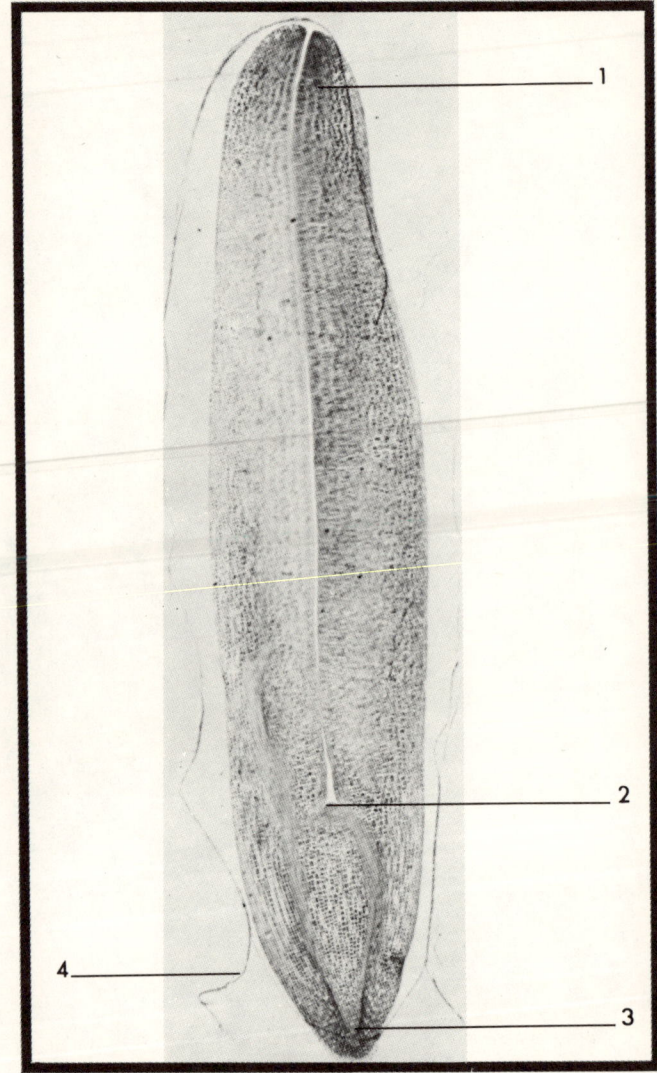

(a) Identify this structure as fully as you can.
(b) List the structures 1 – 4.
(c) Where on the plant does this structure form, and from what?
(d) Where does this structure overwinter in nature?

55.11

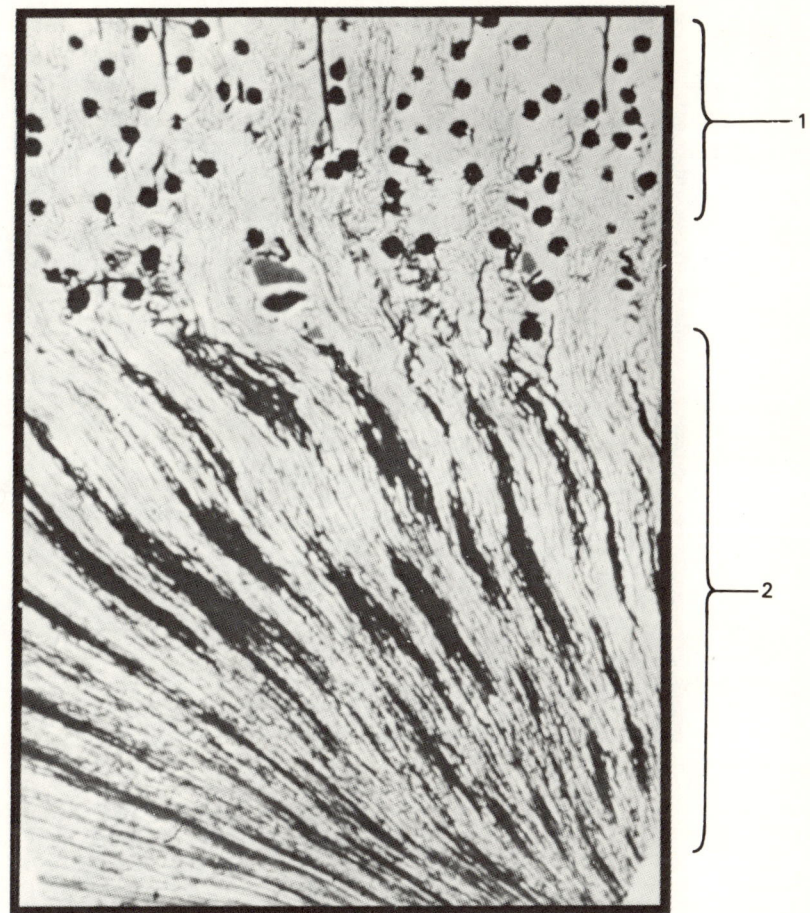

Gene Cox

(a) In the section through the kidney of a mammal list the regions 1 and 2.
(b) Which artery supplies the kidney, and why must the blood be under high pressure for normal kidney tubule function?
(c) State two other sites of excretion in the mammal's body and state what is excreted at each.

55.12

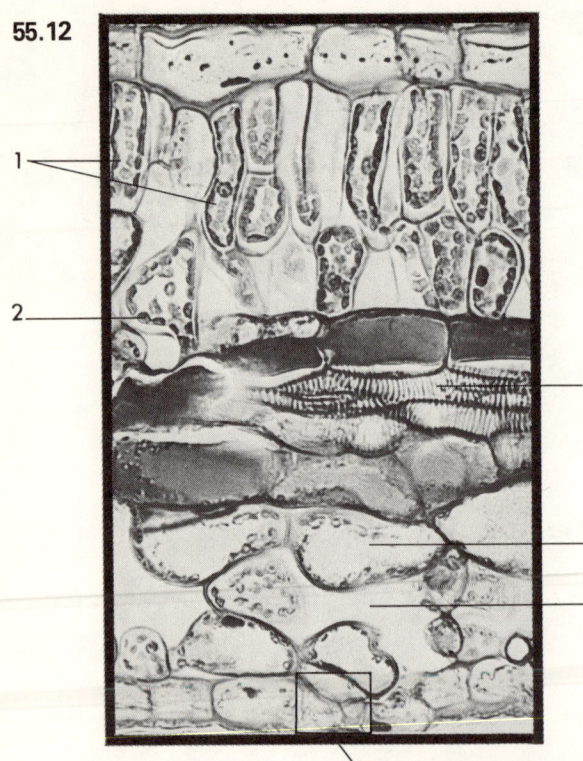

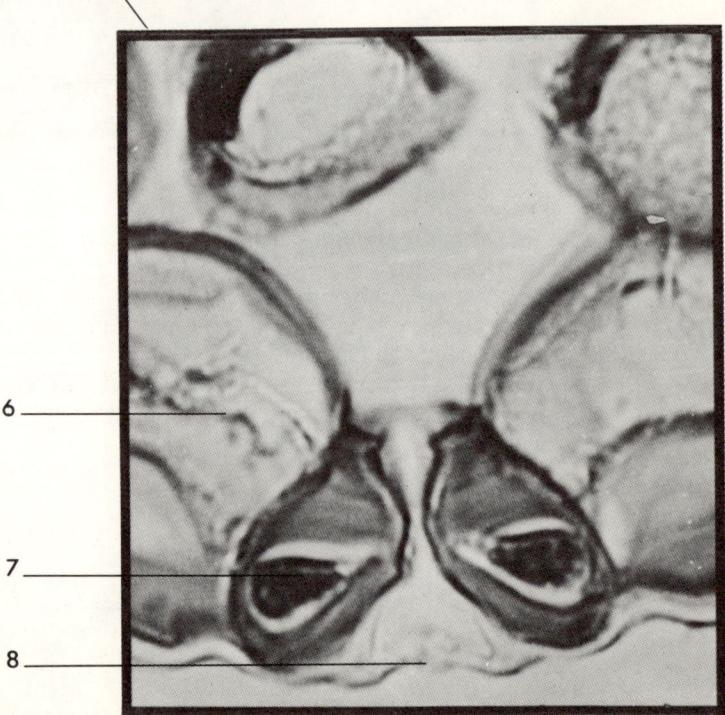

(a) State three structural ways in which the leaf is specialised for photosynthesis.
(b) List the structures 1–5.
(c) What changes occur in cell 6 and in cell 7 when the gap 8 opens.

Gene Cox

55.13 (a) In the Epoxy resin lung the lungs are filled with rubber and all the tissues are digested away with enzymes. List the structures 1 – 4.
(b) What features do lungs have in common with other absorbing surfaces?
(c) What immediate and long-term effects does cigarette smoke have on lung function and structure?

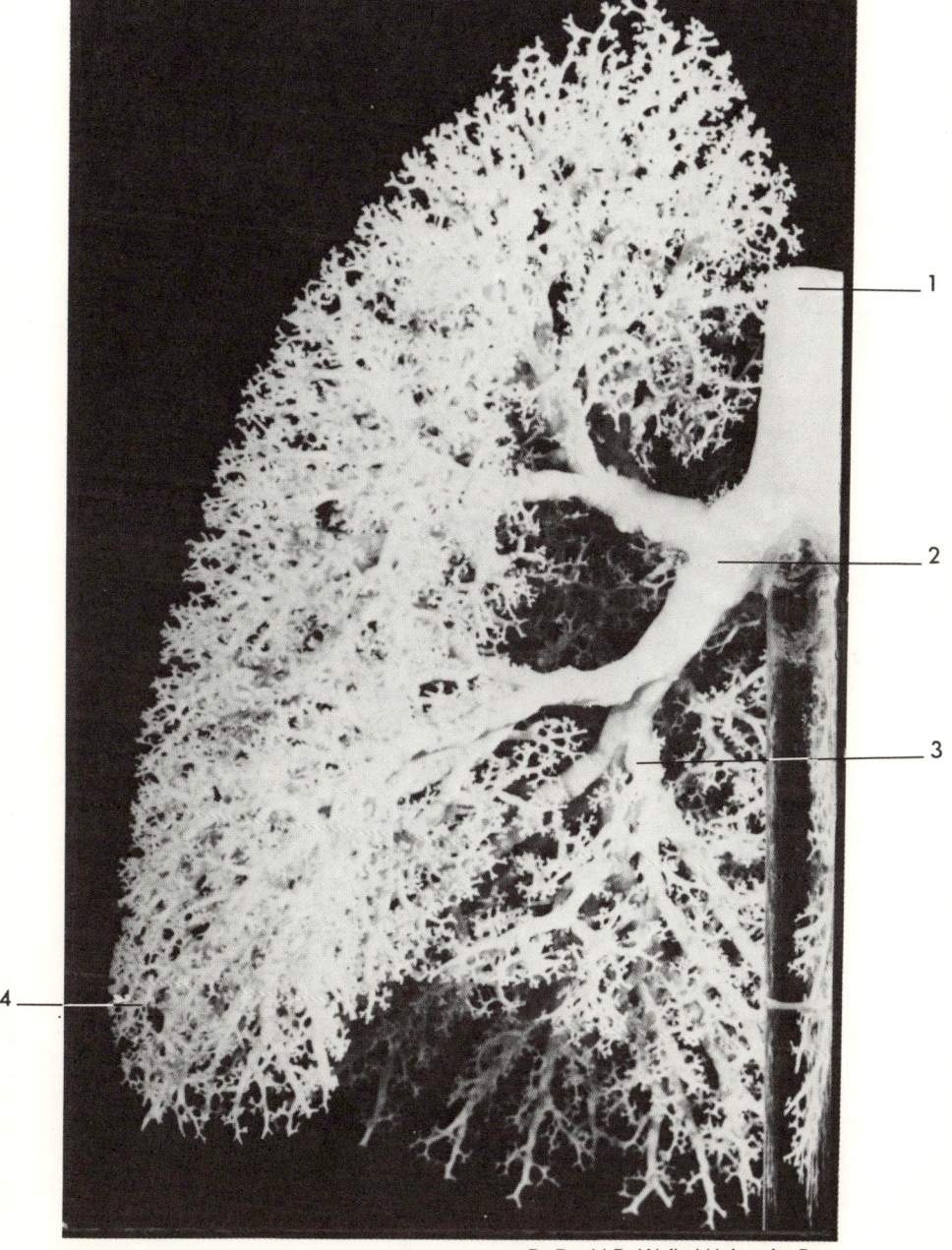

Dr Ewald R. Weibel University Bern

55.14

NHPA

(a) Flower buds on these trees open well before leaf buds break. What advantage does this provide the plant?
(b) What structural features does successful wind-transmitted pollen possess?
(c) Design a stigma to trap this pollen.
(d) Apart from various tree species, which major plant group is wind-pollinated?

55.15

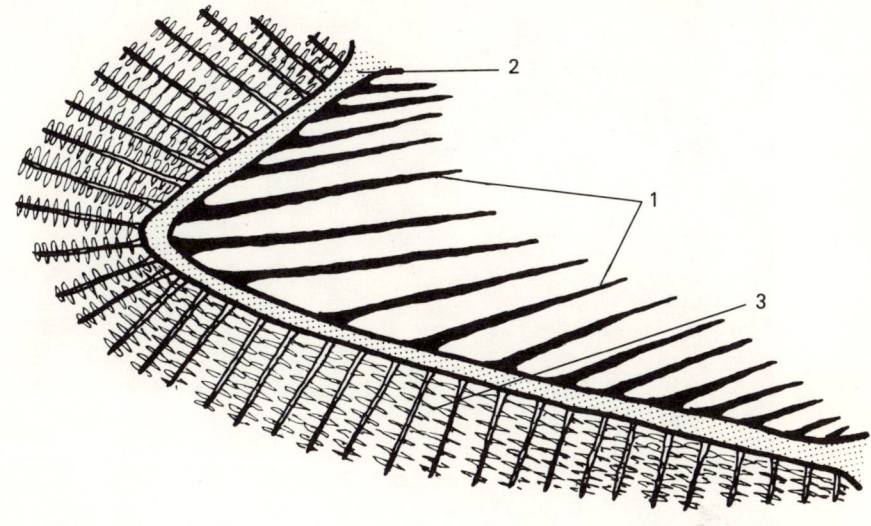

(a) Where does this structure occur in a fish?
(b) List the structures 1 – 3, and state the function of each part.
(c) How is water brought to this structure and moved past it?
(d) How is this structure protected from predators and parasites?

55.16
(a) How do fungi obtain their food?
(b) What substances in the herbivore's dung are these fungi feeding upon?
(c) These fungi explosively propel their spores away from the dung. How do the spores come to occur in fresh dung?

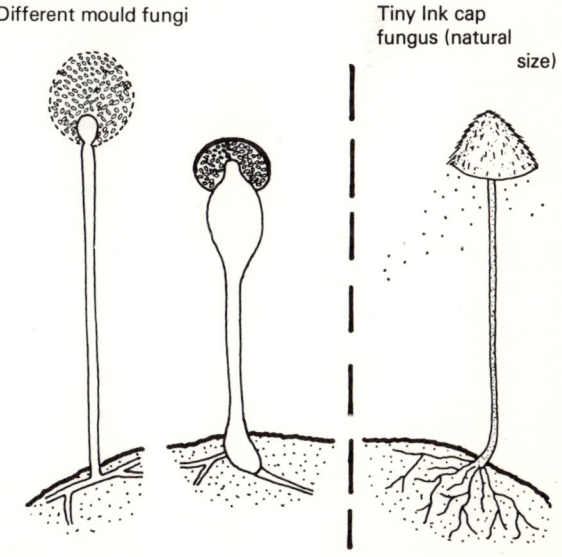

55.17

Howard Jay

(a) List the structures 1 – 4.
(b) What path does the wing tip describe during normal flapping flight?
(c) If the bird were about to land, in what position would the wing and tail be?
(d) What special features of feathers themselves assist the bird in flight?

55.18 (a) List the structures 1 – 7 in the section through a lateral bud and the base of a leaf in autumn.
(b) What change is occurring at 2?
(c) What will 6 appear like in surface view when 3 is removed?
(d) Where else in this section are there protective devices that help the twig overwinter?

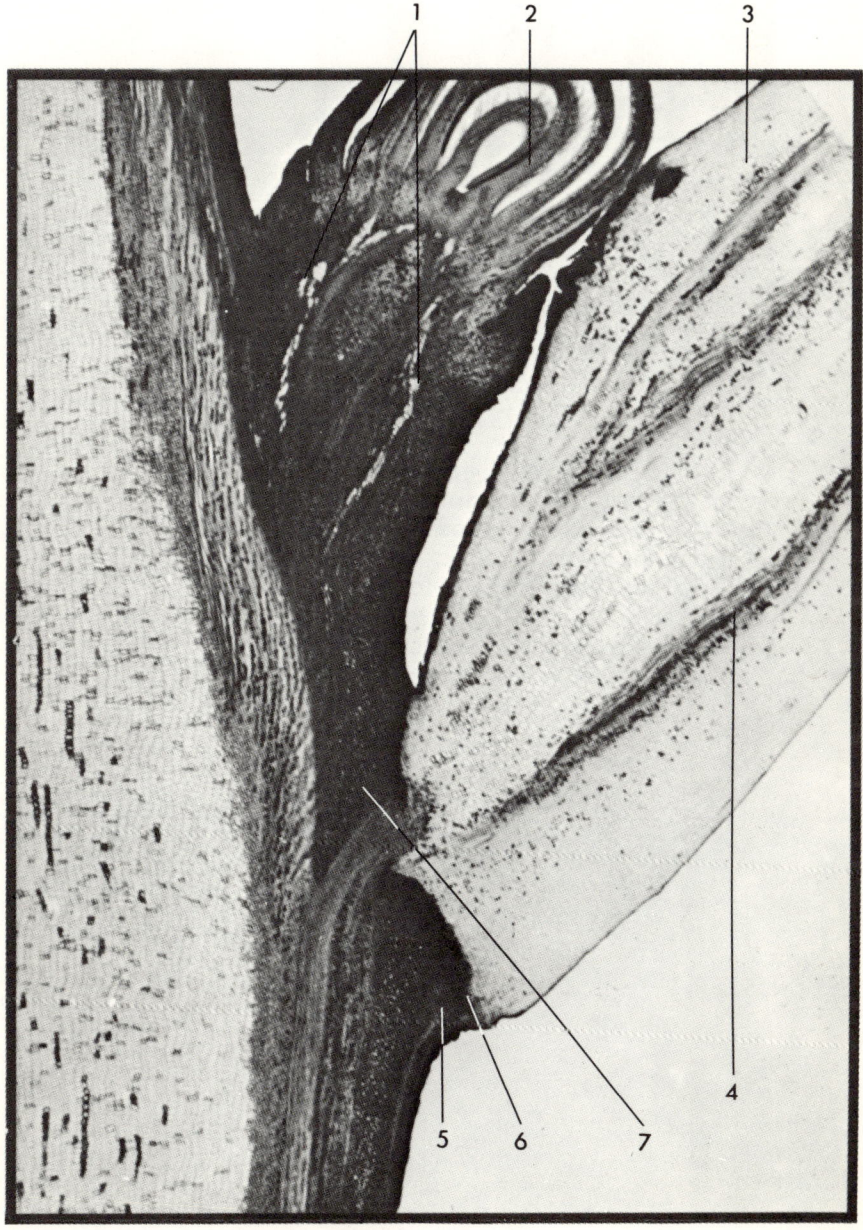

Gene Cox

55.19

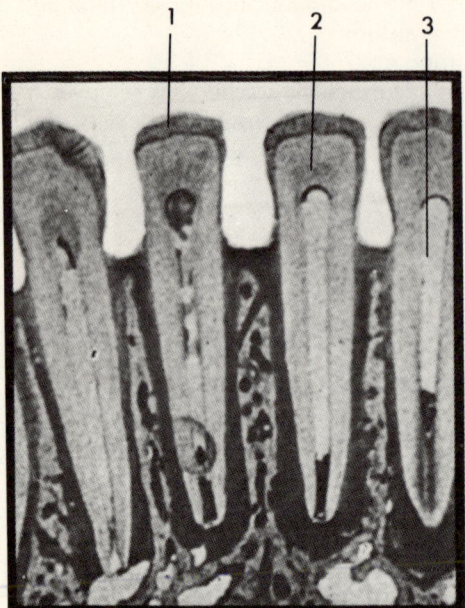

Flatters & Garnett Ltd.

(a) In the section through the incisor teeth of a carnivore list the structures 1 – 3.
(b) What roles do these teeth play in the life of the animal?
(c) How are teeth fixed into the jaw socket?
(d) Suggest two reasons why tooth decay is so prevalent in humans?

55.20

NHPA

(a) What does the insect seek?
(b) What advantage does the plant gain?
(c) What type of relationship do you describe this as?
(d) On what part of the body does the bee receive pollen, and where does it transfer pollen to for flight?
(e) How does a bee 'comb' pollen from its bristles?